SPECIAL COLLECTOR'S EDITION

WINNING ANGRY

WICHITA STATE'S ROAD TO THE 2013 FINAL FOUR

The Wichita Eagle

Kansas.com

Kim Nussbaum, Publisher
Sherry Chisenhall, Editor
John Boogert, Deputy Editor
Tom Shine, Deputy Editor
Kirk Seminoff, Sports Editor
Tom Seals, Assistant Sports Editor
Brian Corn, Photo Editor
Josh Wood, News Editor

Ryan Johnson, Designer
Paul Suellentrop, Reporter
Bob Lutz, Columnist
Tony Adame, Reporter
Travis Heying, Photographer
Jaime Green, Photographer
Fernando Salazar, Photographer
Bo Rader, Senior Photographer

Peter J. Clark, Publisher
Molly Voorheis, Managing Editor
Katherine Grigsby, Layout & Design

ISBN: 978-1-940056-02-9 HC

Printed in the United States of America
KCI Sports Publishing 3340 Whiting Avenue, Suite 5 Stevens Point, WI 54481
Phone: 1-800-697-3756 Fax: 715-344-2668
www.kcisports.com

CONTENTS

WICHITA STATE SHOCKERS

BY PAUL SUELLENTROP

In March 1964, The Wichita Eagle detailed the fan frenzy for Shocker basketball with a story headlined "Cage Town Gone Mad."

Sound familiar? In Wichita, mad and angry mean happy when it comes to hoops.

That description fit Wichita many times over the past 49 years, most notably in 1965 (Final Four), the early 1980s and 2006 (Sweet 16). Wichita long considered itself a "Cage Town." In 2013, it went mad all over again for Shocker basketball and coach Gregg Marshall's Play Angry Express to Atlanta.

Wichita State's 2012-13 season is the story of a team that had to reinvent itself at least three times on its way to the West Regional title and the Final Four. The players say they talked about the Final Four during the summer of 2012. Marshall wished they had told him and saved him a lot of worry during the 18-game grind of the Missouri Valley Conference. Nobody outside the locker room expected a strong NCAA run from the Shockers

The Shockers began to make those predictions look dubious with a 9-0 start that included a win at Virginia Commonwealth, in addition to victories over DePaul, Iowa, Tulsa and Air Force. That 9-0 team didn't get a chance to keep it going. Injuries began to hit, eventually robbing the Shockers of four starters for spans varying from three games (Ehimen Orukpe) to most of the season (Evan Wessel).

With Wessel, Ron Baker (21 games) and Carl Hall (eight games) out in late December, the Shockers retooled for the start of conference play. They kept going with defense and depth. Reserves such as Tekele Cotton and Demetric Williams moved into the starting lineup and thrived. Hall returned in mid-January. WSU started MVC play 8-1, including a win over No. 12 Creighton.

A three-game losing streak started in late January, exposing weaknesses on offense that the Shockers could only survive with total focus on defense. That hard-core devotion to stopping scorers had slipped away, an issue former Shockers Antoine Carr and Xavier McDaniel summed up when they told the Shockers to "Play Angry" before a slump-busting win over Missouri State. Marshall put the season on his seniors and they responded. WSU won five in a row and appeared to claim control of the Valley race. A stunning home loss to Evansville and a loss at Creighton doomed WSU to second place.

Baker's return on March 8 for the quarterfinals of the MVC Tournament remade the Shockers for the final time. Defense and rebounding got them into the NCAA Tournament. Baker's return provided gave the offense enough juice to keep them alive.

WSU beat down Pittsburgh and stunned top-ranked Gonzaga with a hail of three-pointers. It overmatched La Salle and held off Ohio State to advance to the school's first Final Four since 1965. Eventual champion Louisville stopped the Shockers in the national semifinal, but not before they thrilled their fans and proved they belonged with college's basketball's elite.

Coach Gregg Marshall holds the West Regional championship trophy after the Shockers defeated Ohio State.
By Travis Heying, Wichita Eagle

A VISION FOR SUCCESS

MARSHALL BELIEVES WICHITA STATE IS A PLACE TO WIN

BY PAUL SUELLENTROP

G regg Marshall gave his sustainability speech in March 2011, although few realized it. During Wichita State's NIT championship run, he enthusiastically rejected the notion he coaches at a mid-major.

Check my bank account, he said. Check the way my team travels, and the budget, and my talent and the Koch Arena crowd, he challenged. Had that question and answer taken place in the NCAA Tournament, it goes viral and "Check my W-2" becomes a sound bite on ESPN.

With that statement, he signaled his belief in Wichita State's spot in college basketball. Entering his sixth season, he is after a fourth straight 20-win season, something unprecedented for the program.

"I knew coming in, if given time, we could be very successful here because of the renovations to the facility and the great crowd support, which means revenue," he said. "When you eliminate excuses why you can't win, then it's up to you to win. We've got what we need to win."

Marshall and his coaching staff are proving that in landmark numbers. His 2011 team won a school-

WSU's Ehimen Orukpe drives to the basket during a scrimmage. *By Fernando Salazar, Wichita Eagle*

WSU coach Gregg Marshall talks to his team following a scrimmage during Shocker Madness at Koch Arena.
By Fernando Salazar, Wichita Eagle

record 29 games on its way to the NIT championship. The Shockers followed with 27 wins, a Missouri Valley Conference title and an NCAA Tournament appearance in 2012. Those 56 wins are the second-most in MVC history for a two-season span.

WSU, with a history characterized by a decade of success followed by a dropoff, is on a roll with one losing season since 2002. As in the past, success follows the traditional markers.

In the 1950s, the hiring of Ralph Miller and the construction of the WU Fieldhouse (later Levitt Arena and now Koch Arena) opened the door for national rankings and a program-building run in the 1960s. The hiring of Gene Smithson in 1978 fueled the talent-rich 1980s and Eddie Fogler maintained high standards until he departed in 1989.

In 2003, renovated Koch Arena opened for coach Mark Turgeon to power two trips to the NIT and the 2006 Sweet 16. Marshall took over in 2007-08 and needed only two seasons to push the Shockers back into MVC contention.

"We've invested in people," athletic director Eric Sexton said. "We've invested in facilities."

How does Sexton know those investments are paying off? Marshall remains in his Koch Arena office, one increasingly filled with pictures, trophies and souvenirs from Shocker victories, in addition to the ones he brought from Winthrop. If Marshall didn't believe he could win at WSU for years to come, he would find a place more attractive.

"Without a doubt," Marshall said. "I like what we've got going."

While WSU still plays in the shadow of the Big 12, people notice its success nationally. ESPN loves showing games at Koch Arena because of the atmosphere. WSU was the first MVC member to play in the Maui Invitational and it regularly lands spots in good tournaments because of its fan support and reputation.

"Wichita State has a product and a brand," ESPN analyst Jimmy Dykes said. "They play hard. Normal college basketball fans take that for granted or don't understand the importance of that. That's why I like watching them play."

Marshall knows who makes the program go. When he talks recruiting, his voice rises and his speech quickens.

That is why Marshall and assistant coach Chris Jans jumped in a car for a recruiting trip on their way to the Missouri Basketball Coaches Association coaching clinic early last month in Columbia.

They made four stops along the way, a trip reminiscent of his young days as an assistant coach. Marshall did his share of the driving, something not all head coaches are up for. They stopped for enough fast food to keep Jans satisfied - Marshall can go longer without - and the head coach changed clothes in the car to go from clinician to recruiter.

"It was old school," Marshall said. "I saw parts of Missouri that I've never seen. We hit four young kids, and it was great. I don't do that that often anymore."

Marshall does most of his recruiting by airplane these days. In population-poor Kansas, that's a necessity. It is tougher to go on recruiting trips as a family man, but he can't bear to relax.

"When I was 22 years old and they gave me a car and some sunflower seeds and $15 and a credit card for gas and I was good," he said. "I'd drive all over the eastern seaboard. Now, you miss things, the homecoming dance for your son or daughter."

Marshall and his staff understand how to mine the sweet spot in the recruiting world where players are talented enough to play for higher-profile schools while available to an MVC school. He hires assistant coaches with roots across the country and connections to all levels of feeder institutions. He isn't afraid to take chances on academic risks, such as Dayton's Teddy Hawkins, and refuses to get caught short.

Hawkins didn't meet NCAA eligibility standards and is at a prep school in Iowa. His return to WSU, once promised, is iffy after he recently reopened his recruiting. Center Henry Uwadiae, another member of the last fall's signing class, is at a junior college after not meeting NCAA standards.

At many schools, losing two members of a class is devastating. Marshall prepared and filled those scholarships. He finds it funny that fans and the media are concerned about his ability to count to 13 scholarships allowed by the NCAA.

"Towards the end (with Hawkins), we kind of knew where he was and we reacted accordingly,"

Marshall said. "My college coach ... used to say, 'You're only as good as your secondary recruiting list' at some point. That secondary recruiting list better be really good."

This season's roster contains two transfers from Division I schools and five from a junior college. WSU has two Canadians, a Nigerian and a player from the Bahamas. Eight came to WSU from high school, hailing from as close as Wichita and as far as Georgia and Nevada.

"I said the very first day I was hired as head coach that we will recruit locally, regionally, nationally, internationally, universally," Marshall said. "We will look at high schools, prep schools, junior colleges and the military. It doesn't matter, as long as they want to work and work together."

With Marshall satisfied with his resources, sustained success seems likely for WSU. The work started by former athletic director Jim Schaus and Turgeon is continued by Sexton and Marshall.

Sexton thinks the program checks all the major boxes for facilities and amenities. That doesn't mean work stops. WSU is evaluating its locker rooms. A recruiting room, where coaches and administrators meet with athletes and families, is the latest upgrade in recruiting wars to catch Sexton's attention.

A few years ago, it was common to see athletic directors and boosters from other MVC schools touring Koch Arena. Bradley opened a basketball practice facility in 2010. Evansville is opening one this fall and Creighton recently announced plans.

"We made investments in our facility way ahead of many of our competitors in the conference and they are starting to catch up," Sexton said. "We look at those things every year."

Veteran Shocker fans testify that success slips away quickly. Gary Thompson took the 1965 Shockers to the Final Four and exited in 1971 after four losing seasons. Smithson's NBA talent dried up under the weight of NCAA probation and changing times in college basketball. Turgeon's final team plunged from the national rankings to sixth place in the Valley.

Marshall feels confident he can sustain the momentum from three straight 20-win seasons. As he said, there are no excuses.

WSU's Jake White goes up for two during a scrimmage during Shocker Madness at Koch Arena.
By Fernando Salazar, Wichita Eagle

CARL HALL

HALL'S HOMECOMING
DOWN IN COCHRAN, GA., EVERYONE'S A SHOCKER, AND EVERYONE LOVES CARL HALL

BY TONY ADAME

COCHRAN, Ga. -- The house on Peach Street is filling up with people.

There are so many of them, almost all dressed in Wichita State gear, that they spill out the front and side doors, some standing in the yard underneath a slight drizzle of rain and listening to Carl Hall's stepfather, King Fields, as he holds court in the front yard, chain-smoking cigarettes and talking about the Shockers' chances against Louisville on Saturday in the Final Four, just two hours up the road in Atlanta.

Some stand underneath a carport, beneath a sign tacked to the back wall — "Carl Hall #22, Wichita State Shockers, We Are Proud of You!" – and joke about not knowing the person they see on television.

Nobody here calls him Carl, they say. Here, they all call him Tony.

He is, after all, Carl Anthony Hall Jr.

"Who is Carl Hall?" one of his aunts asks. "I'm calling him Tony. I can't call him Carl. He's Tony to me."

Inside the house, Hall's mother, Jackie Fields,

In his senior season, Carl Hall overcame a broken thumb and gave WSU stability inside.
By Fernando Salazar, Wichita Eagle

scrambles from the kitchen to the living room when she hears screaming among the seemingly endless stream of small children running back and forth through the house.

"Nobody better be messing with my baby!" Jackie says. "Nope, nope, nope, y'all ain't doing that. What did y'all do to Tyreke?"

There is laughter from the other room as Jackie comes back into the kitchen carrying her grandson, Carl's 3-year-old son Tyreke, and sits down at the table with him in her lap. Tyreke has been living with Jackie since December.

"Somebody get my baby a cupcake," Jackie says. "You know I will toss each and every one of these little kids up out of here if they're messing with my baby."

The women sitting around the table nod and smile. That's Jackie, they all say. She'll tell you what's on her mind. And don't mess with her kids, or else.

Soon, there will be another baby. Hall and his girlfriend, Elesa Ates, are expecting another boy, due June 1. Doctors have already told her that he might come sooner because he is growing so fast.

The house on Peach Street, deep in the heart of Georgia, is filling up with people.

• • •

If you want to know something about sports in Cochran, John Stanley is probably your guy.

In a town of just over 5,000, John, a long-time assistant boys basketball coach at Bleckley County High, is as well-respected in the community as anyone you'll come across. He's also known Jackie since they were children.

"John is a good man," Jackie said. "He's done a lot for the boys in this town, making sure they don't go to the streets. Not just my boys."

And it was John, with Carl's father in prison for life after a murder conviction, who introduced Carl to sports.

"Here, you're either in sports or you're in the streets," John said. "I've been friends with Jackie almost all my life, so when I saw that (Carl) was old enough, I just grabbed him and pointed him in the direction of sports. At first, he was really quiet and really shy … once he started to out-grow the rest of the kids, that was when he really

started to develop his sense of humor, in part because he excelled at basketball and football and in part so he didn't get picked on."

By the time Carl was in elementary school, the teachers were having a hard time controlling him in class … although he seemed to be able to charm his way out of more trouble then he got into.

"I'd get called up to school from work, telling me I needed to come get Carl," Jackie said. "Then I'd get there and they'd say, 'Oh, never mind, he can stay,' and I just couldn't believe it. 'What'd you call me for in the first place?' He was mischievous, a little hard-headed … he caught a few whippings, that's for sure. A couple of times, I just went and sat in the class with him. He wasn't bad, he was just a big jokester."

Jackie had another son, Tavon Ross, in 1995, and began caring for another boy that was Carl's age, Donja Jackson, after Donja's mother died when he was 10.

And that was their family, through thick and thin.

"You stick together through hard times, you cherish the moments you get with each other," Jackie said. "No matter what, we never lost sight of that."

• • •

Carl always hated the fact that Jackie had to work two and sometimes three jobs to make ends meet. It ate him up on the inside to see her come home, beat, and fall into bed only to wake up and do it all over again.

She babysat when she could. She worked at the hospital at night and at a dentist's office during the day. She cleaned houses. She did home health care.

"He just hated it, he always told me that when he got bigger, he was going to make sure I didn't have to work so much," Jackie said. "And he always worked hard. Always. From the time he was little, helping clean up around the house to when people would start paying him to just do odd jobs."

By the time Carl was 13, he was waking at the crack of dawn to mow yards. By the time the rest of his family woke up, he'd have already knocked out two or three yards.

When the Fourth of July rolled around that year, Jackie was getting ready to have people over when Carl walked in the house from another long day of mowing and she remarked on how much money he'd made.

"I told him he about had enough money to buy his school clothes and he just looked at me like I was speaking another language," Jackie said. "It had never occurred to him that he might be able to do something with that money for himself. He looked at me and said, 'Mama, that money is for you if you need it.'

"I took him to the mall that next day and had him pick out his clothes for the school year. We put them on layaway and he came back and paid them off before school. He was so young, even the people at the store were impressed."

Carl never stopped mowing yards, or working. At the Piggly Wiggly when he got old enough. He kept a little for himself. He gave the rest to Jackie.

"I saw that first hand," Sheri Williams said. "What can you say about a child like that? He loves his mama so much there was nothing he ever did just for himself. It was always the family first."

One Christmas, when Carl was in high school and money was tight, he went to Jackie and forbade her from buying him gifts.

"I heard him talking to mama and he said, 'You better not get me anything, you just get Quanesha and Tavon everything they want,'" Quanesha said. "He didn't even wake up Christmas morning with the rest of us."

Jackie didn't listen. She bought Carl a cell phone and placed it on the pillow next to his head while he was sleeping.

"He always puts us before him," Quanesha said. "That's my brother."

• • •

Carl didn't have the grades to go Division I out of high school, so he enrolled at Middle Georgia, close to home. He played four games his freshman year before he collapsed during a pickup game — the result of a heart condition called neurocardiogenic syncope. It means the heart sometimes beats too fast.

Doctors told him that he could never play basketball again and he went to work on the graveyard shift at Lithonia Lighting in Cochran.

"I worked there for two years in a paint booth, which was very hot … it was a nasty place to work," Carl said. "But it paid the bills."

At the same time, a girl working at the local Dairy Queen caught his eye – Elesa. She was one year younger than Carl at Bleckley High and had just graduated from high school. Elesa's friends and family call her "Tootie" because of how much she resembles a character from the 1980s television show "Facts of Life."

"At first he was coming in once every day, then it was twice, and he was ordering the same thing every time, a large cotton candy Blizzard," Elesa said. "And he was telling everyone I worked with that we were going to start dating. He even bet my manager it was going to take him two weeks … it took a little longer."

Elesa found out she was pregnant at the beginning of 2009 and had Tyreke on Sept. 15, right around the same time medication for Carl's heart condition was giving him hope he could resurrect his basketball career.

It was also then that Carl, previously a lackluster student, started to focus on his future.

"Tyreke changed my life," he said. "He's my reason I wanted to go back to school. I didn't want him growing up not having things, struggling … he motivates me to work hard every day."

Carl dominated at Middle Georgia in 2009-10, leading the Warriors to the Region XVII title and a spot in the NJCAA Tournament in Hutchinson, where he first caught the eye of Wichita State coach Gregg Marshall.

After the season, with doubts that Carl could qualify for Division I because of Georgia's Regents Testing program – required of any junior-college graduate in the state – he transferred to Northwest Florida Community College. The decision caused some static in Cochran, as Carl was part of a mass exodus of players from Middle

Georgia to Florida junior colleges.

At the heart of any story about Carl's transfer, which you can get from almost anyone in Cochran, is Jackie.

"I look out for my children first and foremost," Jackie said. "I make no apologies for that."

Hall signed with Wichita State in November 2010. He averaged 17.6 points and 9.6 rebounds in his one season at Northwest Florida.

• • •

Carl was already well-known in Cochran before the Shockers' run to the Final Four over the last two weeks — he was the Missouri Valley Conference Newcomer of the Year last season and was named to the MVC All-Newcomer team.

This season, he is averaging 12.5 points and 6.9 rebounds and was chosen second-team All-MVC despite missing a month of the season with a broken right thumb.

But the Final Four, two hours north, has created a different kind of buzz in Cochran, where Marshall hit a deer on his way to recruit Carl for the first time.

"I can tell you first-hand how rural it is," Marshall said. "We hit that thing and blew out a tire."

The town itself seems like a little slice of Wichita these days — the Piggly Wiggly has a special Carl Hall cake and Shocker cupcakes. Bleckley County schools superintendent Charlotte Pipkin issued a proclamation changing the school's mascot from the Royals to the Shockers through Monday.

If there's a business in town with some sort of sign or billboard out front, it's got some sort of homage to Carl, mainly wishing him luck.

Everywhere you go it's Carl, Carl, Carl. And don't get them started on his now-famous dreadlocks that he cut off before the NCAA Tournament and mailed to Jackie, who keeps them in a plastic storage bin at her house. Donja, Carl's adopted brother, cut off his own shoulder-length dreadlocks in solidarity the day Wichita State opened NCAA play against Pittsburgh in Salt Lake City.

"You tell these kids who Carl is and they kind of nod their heads and listen to you," Bleckley County athletic director Benji Rogers said. "But when you get Charles Barkley on TV saying 'Carl Hall is a beast,' that changes things a little bit."

Carl smiled when asked what he thought was going on back in his hometown.

"It's a really small town, and the way people treat each other reminds me a lot of Wichita," Carl said. "People look out for each other there. I was one of those kids that was hard-headed and always wanted to do his own thing, so I needed those mentors to kind of guide me through the tough times."

At the Bleckley County Recreation Department, eighth-graders practice a few feet from Hall's framed jersey from Northwest Florida and a team picture of the Shockers.

"The Final Four, everybody knows that's a big deal … as big as it gets," said D.J. Lemmon, 13, who is growing his dreadlocks out just like Hall's were. "And I was shocked when he cut off his hair. Shocked."

• • •

The house on Peach Street is full.

The stories about Carl — Tony — are flying. Some are funny, and people laugh. Some are emotional, and people cry.

"He is the heartbeat of our team," Marshall says on Thursday in Atlanta. "A true warrior."

The last time anyone saw Carl in Cochran was last fall, when he came to town to watch Tavon, a junior, play football. He'll likely come back when the new baby is born. He is contemplating naming him Carl Anthony Hall III.

"That's negotiable," Elesa says, smiling.

"Give that boy his own name!" Sheri says. "He can't!"

Everyone laughs. It is getting deep into the Georgia night. Jackie makes sure everyone has eaten. The women are in the living room and kitchen, talking about Carl.

The men are outside, still discussing whether the Shockers have a shot against Louisville, a conversation that won't end until the game is played on Saturday.

The house on Peach Street is full.

Of so many more things than just the people in it.

BAKER HELPS WSU START ON RIGHT TRACK

BY PAUL SUELLENTROP

R on Baker is calm and matter of fact when he talks about Wichita State basketball. He gets a little more excited talking about his old school, Scott City, in the Class 3A football playoffs.

Perhaps that helps explains why Baker, a redshirt freshman guard, is showing no sign of jitters early in his Shocker career. Playing in front of 10,000 fans is nothing to get excited about when a player shoots as well as Baker. He scored 18 points, making 4 of 7 three-pointers in Saturday's 71-57 win over North Carolina-Central in the opener for both teams.

His teammates aren't surprised. Baker scored 17 points in Monday's exhibition game against Pittsburg State.

"That's what he does - shoot the ball," senior forward Carl Hall said. "You kick it out and you know he's going to hit the shot."

Baker, whose brother Sloan plays special teams for Scott City, redshirted last season so he could prepare for the jump from high school to college. The plan is working so far. In two games, Baker is 8 of 14 from the field, 6 of 12 from the behind the arc, with 10 rebounds. He isn't just a jump shooter, either, if making 13 of 15 free throws is an indication.

WSU's Carl Hall goes up for two against North Carolina Central's Ebuka Anyaorahat.
By Fernando Salazar Wichita Eagle

WSU's Evan Wessel drives against North Carolina Central in the first half at Koch Arena.
By Fernando Salazar Wichita Eagle

"I've been nervous, but mainly I just try and focus," he said. "Redshirting helped out a lot, because I know exactly what is going on during the game and before the game starts. I know the routine. I know what to expect."

Wichita State openers usually feature an over-matched team from a low-profile conference, a lot of substitutions, a few debut jitters and a Shocker victory.

Saturday's win checked all those boxes. Central provided enough resistance with its zone defense and traps to make the Shockers work. Coach Gregg Marshall played a lot of combinations and gave his bench time to work through ups and downs. WSU had no film of the Eagles, so the changing defenses and half-court traps caught them by surprise. The Shockers will see similar strategies - executed more quickly with better athletes - on Tuesday at Virginia Commonwealth.

"This is not really the ideal team to play in your first game, because you don't really have much to scout on," Marshall said. "We weren't prepared for the trap on the first pass. That got us twice."

Central switched to zone and started trapping when it fell behind early. The tactics briefly got the Eagle close.

"We try to multiple defense, especially when you're playing teams with superior athleticism and size just to try to throw them off," Central coach LaVelle Moton said.

Up 12-4, the Shockers turned the ball over five straight times and Central cut the lead to 12-11. It took the Shockers several possessions - and the return of the starters - to slice through the zone and navigate the traps. Hall started a burst with a three-point play for a 19-14 lead. Baker hit back-to-back threes for a 25-14 lead.

With Malcolm Armstead running the offense, things came easier for WSU. He drove into the zone to draw defenders and found Baker open on the baseline for the second of his back-to-back baskets. Baker, who scored 11 first-half points, made another three for a 29-14 lead. WSU's defense carried it through the uncertainty on of-fense. The Eagles missed seven straight shots after closing to within 16-14, most of them contested. WSU held Central to 7-of-26 shooting and forced eight turnovers in the first half. Ehimen Orukpe blocked two shots and altered others.

WSU's Jake White goes up for two against North Carolina Central's Drimir Ferguson.
By Fernando Salazar Wichita Eagle

"We couldn't make shots," Moton said. "They really took us out of what we wanted to do. We have several newcomers, and this was their welcome to col-lege basketball. This is a hostile environment to play your first college game."

WSU led 36-18 at halftime. WSU led by as many as 22 in the second half. The Eagles cut it to 13 late in the game, never seriously threatening. Marshall played 12 players and got a good look at several newcomers and lineups in the second half.

"I thought we were really good in the first half," Marshall said. "In the second half, they outscored us. We've got to live and learn and figure out what to do to get better."

Hall added 17 points, 13 rebounds and three blocks for WSU. He made 9 of 11 free throws. Cleanthony Early came off the bench to score 10 points. Stanton Kidd led Central with 22 points.

BOX SCORE

NC Central 57 • 0-1

##	Player		Total FG-FGA	3-Ptr FG-FGA	FT-FTA	Off	Def	Tot	PF	TP	A	TO	Blk	Stl	Min
01	COPELAND, Jay	f	1-2	0-0	2-4	0	2	2	5	4	0	2	1	0	18
11	KIDD, Stanton	f	8-16	2-3	4-7	5	4	9	4	22	0	2	0	0	40
05	ANYAORAH, Ebuka	g	1-4	0-2	0-0	1	0	1	3	2	1	3	1	0	20
32	CHAPMAN, Emanuel	g	0-2	0-1	0-0	0	4	4	0	0	4	1	0	1	22
55	WILLIS, Ray	g	4-12	2-4	0-1	0	4	4	3	10	4	2	3	1	40
00	FERGUSON, Drimir		0-3	0-0	0-0	0	3	3	0	0	2	0	0	1	19
12	GALAYA, Antonin		0-1	0-1	0-0	0	0	0	0	0	0	0	0	0	1
14	INGRAM, Jeremy		6-15	1-6	3-3	0	2	2	4	16	1	2	0	2	36
40	HOUSTON, Alfonzo		1-1	0-0	1-1	0	0	0	0	3	0	0	0	0	4
	Team					4	1	5							
	Totals		21-56	5-17	10-16	10	20	30	19	57	12	12	5	6	200

FG % 1st Half: 7-26 26.9% 2nd half: 14-30 46.7% Game: 21-56 37.5%
3FG % 1st Half: 0-8 0.0% 2nd half: 5-9 55.6% Game: 5-17 29.4%
FT % 1st Half: 4-4 100.0 2nd half: 6-12 50.0% Game: 10-16 62.5%

Deadball
Rebounds
2

Wichita State 71 • 1-0

##	Player		Total FG-FGA	3-Ptr FG-FGA	FT-FTA	Off	Def	Tot	PF	TP	A	TO	Blk	Stl	Min
22	Hall, Carl	f	4-10	0-0	9-11	6	7	13	2	17	1	1	3	0	28
21	Orukpe, Ehimen	c	2-5	0-0	2-4	5	2	7	3	6	0	2	2	1	16
02	Armstead, Malcolm	g	1-5	0-4	0-0	0	2	2	2	2	6	1	0	1	27
03	Wessel, Evan	g	2-3	1-1	0-0	0	1	1	0	5	3	2	0	0	22
31	Baker, Ron	g	5-8	4-7	4-4	0	4	4	0	18	0	1	0	0	24
00	Lufile, Chadrack		0-0	0-0	0-0	0	3	3	2	0	0	1	0	0	6
05	Williams, Demetric		1-5	0-2	0-0	0	0	0	0	2	3	0	0	0	12
11	Cleanthony Early		5-9	0-1	0-0	3	2	5	1	10	1	1	2	1	22
15	Wiggins, Nick		0-0	0-0	0-2	0	1	1	1	0	1	0	0	0	6
23	VanVleet, Fred		1-3	0-1	0-0	0	4	4	1	2	3	1	0	0	13
32	Cotton, Tekele		2-4	1-1	0-1	1	0	1	1	5	1	0	0	0	15
50	White, Jake		2-4	0-2	0-0	0	2	2	1	4	0	1	0	0	9
	Team					1	1	2							
	Totals		25-56	6-19	15-22	16	29	45	14	71	18	12	7	3	200

FG % 1st Half: 14-27 51.9% 2nd half: 11-29 37.9% Game: 25-56 44.6%
3FG % 1st Half: 5-9 55.6% 2nd half: 1-10 10.0% Game: 6-19 31.6%
FT % 1st Half: 3-7 42.9% 2nd half: 12-15 80.0% Game: 15-22 68.2%

Deadball
Rebounds
2

Officials: Zelton Steed, Don Daily, Hal Lusk
Technical fouls: NC Central-None. Wichita State-None.
Attendance: 10491

Score by periods	1st	2nd	Total
NC Central	18	39	57
Wichita State	36	35	71

WICHITA STATE 53
VCU 51

WSU RESTORES ORDER

SHOCKERS GET WIN OVER VCU'S TOUTED 'HAVOC'

BY PAUL SUELLENTROP

RICHMOND, Va. -- This time, Wichita State made the big plays in the final seconds. Now "Havoc" is just another word, one that doesn't seem so powerful or intimidating as it once did.

WSU, with four players starting their first road game as Shockers, handled VCU's pressure defense and sellout crowd with a 53-51 win at the Siegel Center on Tuesday. Guard Malcolm Armstead sank a 17-foot jumper with 3.8 seconds remaining for the win, ending a game in which he calmly directed WSU's offense against the defense trademarked as "Havoc." WSU survived a miserable shooting night with a series of clutch plays into the teeth of VCU's Rowdy Rams student section.

"He wanted it, and I was smart enough to listen," WSU coach Gregg Marshall said. "It worked pretty well."

Armstead's shot almost quieted the crowd. Then the Shockers had to survive a scare when Carl Hall fouled Juvonte Reddic in the final second. Reddic's first free throw spun out. He missed the second one off the backboard, a violation that

Wichita State's Carl Hall blocks a shot by VCU's Juvonte Reddic in the second half. Wichita State won, 53-51.
By P. Kevin Morley, Richmond Times-Dispatch

Wichita State's Cleanthony Early shoots with VCU's Juvonte Reddic defending in the second half at VCU's Siegel Center.
By P. Kevin Morley, Richmond Times-Dispatch

gave the ball to WSU with 0.5 seconds to play. A quick inbound pass erased some of the frustration from a 68-67 loss to VCU in 2011 in Koch Arena and March's 62-59 loss in the NCAA Tournament.

The Shockers didn't play like a team that lost five seniors from 2011-12. Freshman, sophomores, newcomers - they all showed remarkable calm and composure in pressure-packed environment. Junior transfer Cleanthony Early came off the bench to score 13 points. Armstead, playing his first road game as a Shocker after sitting out last season, scored 11 points and had six assists and four steals.

"I felt like everybody seemed experienced," WSU redshirt freshman Ron Baker said. "I don't have any late-game experience, but it really felt

like everybody was in that mode."

Before Tuesday's game, WSU coaches told their players to embrace the way VCU played and take advantage. The Shockers did some of that, breaking the press and making open shots. They also hit the Rams with their own tough defense to hand VCU its first November home loss since 2002.

"They did a good job dealing with our press and our crowd and the way we play," VCU coach Shaka Smart said. "They certainly were not scared."

Certainly not Armstead.

With the game tied 51-all, WSU got the ball with 26.6 seconds to play. The Shockers flattened

Wichita State coach Gregg Marshall shouts instructions in the second half.
By P. Kevin Morley, Richmond Times-Dispatch

out four players along the baseline to give Armstead room. He waved off a ball screen and went at VCU's Briante Weber. When Weber gave ground, Armstead swished a long jumper for a 53-51 lead.

"He backed up a lot, so I gave him a hesitation, which he bit for, and I rose up," Armstead said. "I'm tired, I'm sick, but I feel good though."

Armstead's winner capped a series of clutch plays that gave WSU a bit of space in a physical, grinding defensive effort.

Demetric Williams found Carl Hall with a pretty bounce pass for a layup and 45-44 lead with 2:03 remaining. Early scored after a VCU turnover for a 47-44 lead. Then the big one - the Shockers fought off traps and reversed the ball to Early for a dunk and a 49-45 lead.

WSU shot 35.1 percent from the field, missing 16 of 19 threes. They limited turnovers to 13, four in the second half, and never let the Rams go on big runs. VCU shot 34.7 percent from the field and missed 12 of 24 foul shots.

"This is third time we've played them in three years, and every year they've done a nice job against the press," Smart said. "Tonight served as a reminder that we have a long way to go. If we're not on edge and playing the way that we need to play, in terms of our approach, teams can beat us. Some of our guys may have lost sight of that."

VCU's press turned the game briefly in the second half. WSU committed turnovers on its first three possessions and the Rams scored after each to build a 33-28 lead. WSU finally broke through with Armstead's runner of the glass.

WSU refused to fold, even as the crowd roared

and the Rams tried to pick up the pressure. Baker broke VCU's momentum with a three-pointer, after freeing himself with a pump fake that sent a defender soaring by. His basket tied it 33-all.

"Marshall warned us that we were going to handle adversity before the game, and he brought it up again on the bench," Baker said. "He challenged us as a unit to attack the adversity and get through it."

Wichita State's Malcolm Armstead tries to pass under pressure from VCU's Briante Weber.
By P. Kevin Morley, Richmond Times-Dispatch

BOX SCORE

WSU 53 • 2-0

##	Player		Total FG-FGA	3-Ptr FG-FGA	FT-FTA	Rebounds Off	Def	Tot	PF	TP	A	TO	Blk	Stl	Min
02	Armstead, Malcolm	*	5-12	0-4	1-3	0	5	5	3	11	6	3	0	4	33
03	Wessel, Evan	*	1-3	1-3	0-0	0	1	1	2	3	0	1	0	0	19
21	Orukpe, Ehimen	*	0-0	0-0	2-2	0	1	1	2	2	0	1	2	0	16
22	Hall, Carl	*	6-15	0-0	0-1	7	4	11	4	12	0	0	3	0	36
31	Baker, Ron	*	3-8	2-7	1-2	2	0	2	2	9	0	1	0	1	28
00	Lufile, Chadrack		0-0	0-0	0-0	0	0	0	0	0	0	0	0	0	0+
05	Williams, Demetric		1-4	0-0	0-0	0	2	2	2	2	1	1	0	2	23
11	Cleanthony Early		4-10	0-4	5-6	3	3	6	3	13	0	3	2	0	23
23	VanVleet, Fred		0-1	0-0	0-0	0	2	2	0	0	1	3	0	1	5
32	Cotton, Tekele		0-4	0-1	1-2	1	3	4	2	1	0	0	0	0	16
50	White, Jake		0-0	0-0	0-0	0	1	1	0	0	1	0	0	0	1
	Team					1	2	3							
	Totals		20-57	3-19	10-16	14	24	38	20	53	9	13	7	8	200

FG % 1st Half: 10-28 35.7% 2nd half: 10-29 34.5% Game: 20-57 35.1%
3FG % 1st Half: 2-12 16.7% 2nd half: 1-7 14.3% Game: 3-19 15.8%
FT % 1st Half: 6-9 66.7% 2nd half: 4-7 57.1% Game: 10-16 62.5%

Deadball Rebounds 4

VCU 51 • 1-1

##	Player		Total FG-FGA	3-Ptr FG-FGA	FT-FTA	Rebounds Off	Def	Tot	PF	TP	A	TO	Blk	Stl	Min
10	THEUS, Darius	*	4-11	2-4	5-8	0	1	1	2	15	5	3	0	2	35
15	REDDIC, Juvonte	*	8-11	0-0	6-9	5	5	10	2	22	1	4	1	2	33
21	GRAHAM, Treveon	*	1-7	1-2	0-2	0	1	1	4	3	1	2	0	0	21
30	DANIELS, Troy	*	2-5	2-4	0-0	1	5	6	1	6	0	0	0	2	31
33	HALEY, D.J.	*	1-1	0-0	0-0	1	2	3	1	2	0	0	1	0	14
02	WEBER, Briante		0-2	0-1	0-0	0	4	4	3	0	3	4	0	0	20
05	OKEREAFOR Teddy		0-1	0-0	0-0	0	2	2	0	0	0	0	0	0	6
11	BRANDENBERG, Rob		1-7	0-2	1-2	0	2	2	1	3	1	0	0	1	26
23	GUEST, Jarred		0-3	0-0	0-0	2	1	3	1	0	0	1	0	1	11
32	JOHNSON, Melvin		0-1	0-1	0-2	0	0	0	0	0	0	0	0	1	3
	Team					4	2	6				1			
	Totals		17-49	5-14	12-23	13	25	38	15	51	11	15	2	9	200

FG % 1st Half: 8-26 30.8% 2nd half: 9-23 39.1% Game: 17-49 34.7%
3FG % 1st Half: 3-7 42.9% 2nd half: 2-7 28.6% Game: 5-14 35.7%
FT % 1st Half: 5-12 41.7% 2nd half: 7-11 63.6% Game: 12-23 52.2%

Deadball Rebounds 6

Officials: Scott Thornley, Randy Heimerman, Jeff Campbell
Technical fouls: WSU-None. VCU-None.
Attendance: 7693

Score by periods	1st	2nd	Total
WSU	28	25	**53**
VCU	24	27	**51**

WICHITA STATE 75
IOWA   63

WSU PLAYING TO ITS STRENGTHS

BY PAUL SUELLENTROP

CANCUN, Mexico -- Wichita State's men's basketball team will stay at the Moon Palace Resort until Saturday. After playing six games in 12 days, the Shockers are ready for a brief vacation.

Wednesday's 75-63 win over Iowa in the Cancun Challenge's Riviera Division earned WSU its first tournament championship away from its home arena since 1963. Its first 6-0 start since 2006-07 is earning it some national respect. Seth Davis of CBS and Sports Illustrated called the Shockers the big early surprise in a Thanksgiving Twitter message - "Whole new team yet won at VCU and beat DePaul & Iowa to win Cancun Challenge."

With its pre-Christmas non-conference schedule halfway finished, WSU certainly exceeded external expectations for a team with four new starters. They own an impressive road win (VCU) and double-digit victories over the Big East (DePaul, picked near the bottom of the 15-team conference) and the Big 10 (Iowa, picked near the middle of the 12-team conference). On Monday, WSU received 13 votes in the Associated Press poll (none in the ESPN/USA Today coaches poll) and that number will rise next week.

"This team, man, is resilient," WSU coach Gregg Marshall said. "It's a special group. I'm re-

The Wichita State Shockers hold the championship trophy after defeating Iowa in Cancun, Mexico.
By Brian Petrotta, Wichita State Athletics

ally excited that they're playing so well right now, and I know they can play even better. I'm not saying we're a top 25 team, but we've got to be in the conversation."

Wichita State's Carl Hall shoots a free throw during the Cancun Challenge championship game. Hall scored 12 points in the Shockers' 75-63 victory. *By Brian Petrotta, Wichita State Athletics*

Six games revealed several items, most of them positive.

The roster turnover hasn't been a problem, yet, largely because of WSU's experienced guards.

Malcolm Armstead controls the game on offense with his quickness and ball-handling. Demetric Williams pairs with Armstead as disruptive forces on defense. Williams set the stage for the win at VCU with his physical defense on the Rams guards. Armstead is slicing up any team silly enough to press and scoring when needed. With those two playing well, WSU's younger guards are protected.

"(Armstead's) got a special talent for getting through (defenses) and making plays," Marshall said.

The Shockers are winning with defense. DePaul shot 30.6 percent, making 15 baskets.

Iowa shot 26.1 percent, making 12 baskets. For the season, opponents are shooting 35.9 percent from the field and 34 percent from three-point range.

While WSU's guards are skilled at bullying ball-handlers, the big men are stop signs in the lane. Ehimen Orukpe blocked five shots against Iowa and has 12 this season. Carl Hall has 10 and Cleanthony Early six. With Orukpe in their heads, Iowa scored six points in the paint.

"He almost has more of an effect when he's not blocking them because you're wondering where he is, and you're looking for him and you shot-fake and you're looking around," Iowa coach Fran McCaffery said. "He affected a lot more than that (five blocks)."

The defensive downside is fouling. WSU committed 57 fouls in Cancun, leading to a 21-point

The Wichita State Shockers hold the championship trophy after defeating Iowa 75-63 in the Cancun Challenge title game in Cancun, Mexico. *By Brian Petrotta,Wichita State Athletics*

disadvantage at the foul line.

WSU's offense either rises to the occasion or is inconsistent. Take your pick.

The Shockers are shooting 42.9 percent from the field and 28.1 percent from three-point range. But the Shockers are capable of better, as they showed by scoring 48 points in the second half against DePaul and 42 against Iowa. The outside shooting nudged up to an acceptable clip against the Hawkeyes when WSU made 7 of 20 (35.1 percent). Armstead and Cleanthony Early, both 1 of 12 from three entering the game, found their stroke. Armstead made 3 of 5 and Early made 3 of 6.

WSU's careful ball-handling (13.5 turnovers a game) and free throw shooting (72 percent) can cover up some poor shooting.

Early's continued development can change this picture. He is averaging a team-leading 14 points and making 48.3 percent of his shots. At 6-foot-8, he has offensive skills rarely seen around the Missouri Valley Conference. While the Shockers aren't shooting the ball accurately yet, they appear to possess a number of good scoring options.

Depth will again be a strength.

Early is giving WSU a dynamic scorer off the bench. He torched the Hawkeyes for 25 points. He and Williams are the constants off the bench, both playing starter minutes. Against DePaul, sopho-

more forward Jake White picked up for Early's foul troubles and scored six points and grabbed three rebounds in a season-high 17 minutes. Against Iowa, sophomore guard Tekele Cotton had five rebounds, three steals and scored eight points in 16 minutes. When Williams struggled with turnovers, freshman Fred VanVleet calmly ran the team for a few minutes.

"We're on the same page and we're tough as nails," Cotton said. "If we stick together and keep doing what we're doing right now, it's going to be hard to beat us."

Wichita State's Cleanthony Early shoots a free throw in Cancun, Mexico. Early scored 25 points against Iowa.
By Brian Petrotta, Wichita State Athletics

BOX SCORE

Iowa 63 • 5-1

##	Player		Total FG-FGA	3-Ptr FG-FGA	FT-FTA	Off	Def	Tot	PF	TP	A	TO	Blk	Stl	Min
15	McCabe, Zach	f	0-3	0-1	0-0	0	1	1	4	0	0	1	0	0	13
30	White, Aaron	f	1-4	1-2	11-12	0	3	3	3	14	1	2	1	2	35
34	Woodbury, Adam	c	0-3	0-0	1-3	1	0	1	3	1	1	0	1	0	17
04	Marble, Roy Devyn	g	4-12	2-2	1-2	3	1	4	2	11	2	5	0	0	36
10	Gesell, Mike	g	0-3	0-0	2-2	1	2	3	4	2	0	3	0	0	12
00	Olaseni, Gabriel		0-0	0-0	0-0	0	0	0	0	0	0	0	0	0	3
01	Basabe, Melsahn		0-2	0-0	6-8	0	2	2	2	6	0	1	1	0	21
02	Oglesby, Josh		4-11	4-8	0-0	0	5	5	2	12	1	1	2	0	21
05	Clemmons, Anthony		1-1	1-1	0-0	0	2	2	1	3	1	0	0	0	11
24	Ingram, Pat		0-1	0-0	1-2	0	0	0	0	1	1	0	0	0	8
25	May, Eric		2-6	0-1	9-10	2	4	6	1	13	0	1	0	0	23
	Team					3	0	3							
	Totals		12-46	8-15	31-39	10	20	30	22	63	7	14	5	2	200

FG % 1st Half: 8-22 36.4% 2nd half: 4-24 16.7% Game: 12-46 26.1%
3FG % 1st Half: 7-8 87.5% 2nd half: 1-7 14.3% Game: 8-15 53.3%
FT % 1st Half: 12-15 80.0% 2nd half: 19-24 79.2% Game: 31-39 79.5%

Deadball Rebounds 5,3

Wichita State 75 • 6-0

##	Player		Total FG-FGA	3-Ptr FG-FGA	FT-FTA	Off	Def	Tot	PF	TP	A	TO	Blk	Stl	Min
22	Hall, Carl	f	3-6	0-0	6-7	2	2	4	4	12	0	2	1	0	21
21	Orukpe, Ehimen	c	2-2	0-0	0-0	2	6	8	3	4	0	1	5	1	23
02	Armstead, Malcolm	g	4-12	3-5	3-5	2	3	5	4	14	5	2	1	4	30
03	Wessel, Evan	g	1-3	1-2	0-0	0	1	1	3	3	1	0	0	0	16
31	Baker, Ron	g	0-7	0-4	2-2	0	1	1	2	2	1	0	0	0	28
00	Lufile, Chadrack		1-1	0-0	0-0	0	0	0	2	2	0	0	1	0	4
05	Williams, Demetric		0-1	0-0	0-0	0	1	1	2	0	3	2	0	0	17
11	Early, Cleanthony		7-13	3-6	8-9	4	5	9	4	25	1	4	0	1	30
15	Wiggins, Nick		2-3	0-1	0-1	0	2	2	0	4	0	0	0	0	5
23	VanVleet, Fred		0-1	0-0	1-2	0	0	0	1	1	1	0	0	0	8
32	Cotton, Tekele		3-4	0-1	2-3	2	3	5	0	8	1	0	0	3	16
50	White, Jake		0-2	0-1	0-0	1	0	1	1	0	0	0	0	0	2
	Team					1	0	1				1			
	Totals		23-55	7-20	22-29	14	24	38	26	75	13	12	8	9	200

FG % 1st Half: 9-23 39.1% 2nd half: 14-32 43.8% Game: 23-55 41.8%
3FG % 1st Half: 4-10 40.0% 2nd half: 3-10 30.0% Game: 7-20 35.0%
FT % 1st Half: 11-14 78.6% 2nd half: 11-15 73.3% Game: 22-29 75.9%

Deadball Rebounds 2,3

Officials: Bill Ek, Darryl Smith, Jim Schipper
Technical fouls: Iowa-None. Wichita State-None.
Attendance: 902
2012 Triple Crown Sports Cancun Challenge

Score by periods	1st	2nd	Total
Iowa	35	28	63
Wichita State	33	42	75

DEMETRIC WILLIAMS

AN ORDERLY CAREER
SENIOR WILLIAMS HELPS KEEP SHOCKERS IN THE RIGHT PLACE

BY PAUL SUELLENTROP

Neatness and order are important to Wichita State guard Demetric Williams, so much so he jokes it is a borderline compulsion for him.

His T-shirts are folded and divided by color in his closet at home. His Koch Arena locker is the neatest in the room, with knee braces folded, watch and wallet stacked on a shelf, clothes hanging precisely and practice gear draped over the chair.

"One time I came to my locker and my shoes were not in the right spot," he said. "I was yelling 'Who was by my locker and moved my shoes?' Everything has got to be where I put it, in the right order."

There are times when Williams doesn't mind making a mess, always one that somebody else needs to fix. When the Shockers are at their best, it is Williams leading a frenzied defense with his quickness and sticky hands. It reminds older brother Thomas Harris of growing up in Las Vegas, when Williams would invade Harris' room and create disorder.

"As a kid, he was messy," Harris said. "We

WSU's Demetric Williams drives to the basket against Creighton. Williams finished his career playing in a school-record 140 games.
By Fernando Salazar, Wichita Eagle

would always fight, because I would say 'I cleaned my room and you come in here and play touch football in my room. It's not a football field. You're knocking everything over.' "

Williams is one of four Shocker seniors who will play their final home game Wednesday against Evansville (16-13, 8-8 Missouri Valley Conference). WSU (24-5, 12-4) can clinch a share of the Valley title with a win. Should second-place Creighton lose at Bradley on Wednesday, WSU can win it outright.

The fact WSU is in this position is a tribute to Williams and the other seniors - forward Carl Hall, center Ehimen Orukpe and guard Malcolm Armstead. When the Shockers lost three in a row, coach Gregg Marshall put the season on the seniors and told them their legacy hung in the balance. Williams, WSU's lone four-year senior, made contributions nobody else could because of his length of service. He talked more in the locker room and in practice. He played hurt, dealing with a bruised hip. Marshall calls him totally focused during games, always making eye contact and giving full attention to instruction. WSU is 5-0 since Marshall put the four seniors in the starting lineup, and 40 minutes from winning back-to-back MVC titles.

"There are times in his career when he's been distant," Marshall said. "These last several weeks, he has been engaged and locked in - the term I use is 'In a great place.' He's tremendous playing his role."

The three-game losing streak in late January and early February hit Williams in ways it couldn't hit the other seniors. He owns 105 wins, more than any other Shocker in program history. More than anybody else in the locker room, he understood the sacrifices made to climb to the top of the Valley the past four years. The losses to Indiana State, Northern Iowa and Southern Illinois pushed him out of his comfort zone. He became the team spokesman, always telling people the Shockers expected to win the conference title and he didn't want that standard to slip.

"He was kind of playing along since we were winning," freshman guard Fred VanVleet said. "Then we hit that streak of three games and he said 'Wait a minute. I haven't lost too many.' It hit home

for him. He's definitely stepped it up since then."

Williams played as a freshman and sophomore, but it took until his junior season for him to thrive. He started 23 games and earned Marshall's trust by playing under control, eliminating turnovers and excelling on defense.

"He found his niche and really does a great job helping his team win," Marshall said. "His greatest strength is also, sometimes, his greatest weakness, and that is his competitive nature. He really likes to compete. Sometimes, it gets to be a little too much and it gets in his way - but rarely."

Williams also sees his junior year as a turning point in school. As a freshman and sophomore, he was happy to get by. When an academic adviser went out of her way to praise him for an acceptable grade on a paper his junior year, he questioned the compliment, asking "Would you praise (former Shocker) Garrett Stutz for that grade?" Williams no longer wanted to be treated like an athlete who couldn't be trusted to do his homework. He wanted to be treated like a student, one who could take responsibility and didn't expect people to celebrate him doing the basics.

"I felt like it was something I was supposed to do, so it's not something I'm supposed to get praised on because I did good this one time," he said. "It's something I've got to keep doing. I'm supposed to come here to get my education. I'm supposed to do good in school. When I was a freshman and sophomore, I probably would have been happy. It's part of growing up."

Williams isn't sure how he will handle his emotions running out of the Koch Arena tunnel for a final time. Harris will watch his first Shocker game, along with other family on Wednesday. As he accompanied Williams to weights and watched practice Tuesday, he often heard Williams talk about the realization his time in Koch Arena's gyms, locker rooms and weight rooms is drawing to a close.

"I'm excited, I'm anxious," Williams said. "I'm also a little sad that my four years came so fast. All the other seniors told me it was going to be come by so fast. I'm just so blessed and happy that I've been able to finish my four years healthy and been able to turn this program around."

WICHITA STATE 86
TULSA 60

HEALTHY MARGIN

SICK AND INJURED SHOCKERS BLOW PAST TULSA

BY PAUL SUELLENTROP

Wednesday's Wichita State shootaround looked ominous, with the bench full of sick and injured big men. Coach Gregg Marshall pondered four-guard lineups and hoped for doctors and trainers to work their magic.

By tip-off, the Shockers looked healthy and they played that way in an 86-60 win over Tulsa at Koch Arena. WSU won its fifth straight over its oldest rival with season's best shooting performances of 52.2 percent and 36.8 percent from three-point range.

WSU's leading scorers watched shootaround, not looking particularly energetic.

Forward Carl Hall fought a vomit-inducing virus. Forward Cleanthony Early strained a ligament in his left ankle in Tuesday's practice and Marshall considered him a scratch until an hour before the game. Hall scored 16 points and grabbed 11 rebounds. Early added 13 points. Center Chadrack

Right: WSU's Tekele Cotton dunks the ball on Tulsa's Shaquille Harrison at Koch Arena.
By Fernando Salazar, Wichita Eagle

Facing Page: WSU's Ron Baker drives on Tulsa's Shaquille Harrison in the first half.
By Fernando Salazar, Wichita Eagle

Lufile felt sick on Tuesday and played 14 solid minutes Wednesday. Center Ehimen Orukpe is out with a sprained right ankle. He watched from the bench wearing a walking boot.

"I can play sick," Hall said. "I played football in cold weather. It's nothing to play in the gym."

With so few feeling great, everybody pitched in for the Shockers (7-0). Nine players played 14 or more minutes, nobody more than 26. Six players scored eight or more points, with the reserves outscoring Tulsa's bench 36-13. Freshman guard Fred VanVleet scored nine points, adding five assists and four steals in his best performance in college. Guard Tekele Cotton made hustle plays in the first half, a two-handed dunk off an inbound play in the second, and scored eight points for the second straight game.

"I didn't know who we would have," Marshall said. "We were going to play a very small lineup. So the doctors and the trainers ... they're the MVP."

Tulsa (4-3) had its own problems. New coach Danny Manning missed injured starter Rashad Smith and started three freshmen. The Golden Hurricane gave up a 12-4 run to end the first half and a 13-2 run midway through the second. WSU's experience and size gave it an edge on the backboard and defensively.

Freshman James Woodard led Tulsa with 14 points. The Hurricane committed 16 turnovers, leading to 24 WSU points.

"We weren't able to match their energy," Manning said. "We competed a little bit, but across the board we have to do a better job of competing, especially on the glass. They got too many second-chance opportunities."

WSU put the game away with a second-half burst that expanded its lead to 72-50. Hall scored five points during that run and brought fans to their feet with a chasedown block to deny Tulsa's Kauri Black a layup.

"We picked up the pressure on the ball," VanVleet said. "I noticed that they were kind of weak

with the ball on the perimeter, so I wanted to get up in them a little bit. We forced a couple steals and got some stops."

Cotton's hustle sparked the Shockers early in the game. He grabbed two offensive rebounds and scored three points.

The Shockers broke free of Tulsa's slow pace late in the first half. Malcolm Armstead broke a half-court press to make an open three-pointer for a 21-15 lead. Wessel followed with another three. Hall's three-point play with 3:22 remaining started a 7-0 run to give WSU a 33-23 lead. Early scored six of WSU's final nine points in the half.

VanVleet's three in the final seconds put WSU up 38-27 at halftime. WSU surprised Tulsa with a press to start the second half. A turnover led to Wessel's three, part of a 9-2 run to open the half.

BOX SCORE

Tulsa 60 • 4-3

##	Player		Total FG-FGA	3-Ptr FG-FGA	FT-FTA	Off	Def	Tot	PF	TP	A	TO	Blk	Stl	Min
00	BLACK, Kauri	f	4-6	0-0	1-4	3	2	5	5	9	1	1	1	0	23
40	WRIGHT, D'Andre	f	3-6	0-0	1-3	3	5	8	4	7	1	0	0	0	19
10	WOODARD, James	g	6-13	1-5	2-3	2	4	6	4	15	1	4	0	0	28
11	HARRISON, Shaquille	g	2-9	0-1	3-4	0	6	6	0	7	1	4	1	1	34
34	HARALSON, Scottie	g	3-8	3-7	0-0	0	1	1	0	9	1	0	0	2	34
03	RAY, Rashad		2-7	1-4	2-2	0	1	1	2	7	1	2	1	1	29
05	PEETE, Tim		1-3	0-1	2-2	0	2	2	2	4	3	3	0	2	18
15	KING, Zeldric		1-2	0-0	0-0	0	0	0	1	2	0	2	0	0	15
	Team					1	5	6							
	Totals		22-54	5-18	11-18	9	26	35	18	60	9	16	3	6	200

FG % 1st Half: 11-28 39.3% 2nd half: 11-26 42.3% Game: 22-54 40.7%
3FG % 1st Half: 1-7 14.3% 2nd half: 4-11 36.4% Game: 5-18 27.8%
FT % 1st Half: 4-6 66.7% 2nd half: 7-12 58.3% Game: 11-18 61.1%

Deadball Rebounds 2

Wichita State 86 • 7-0

##	Player		Total FG-FGA	3-Ptr FG-FGA	FT-FTA	Off	Def	Tot	PF	TP	A	TO	Blk	Stl	Min
11	Early, Cleanthony	f	6-15	1-5	0-0	3	1	4	3	13	1	0	0	1	26
22	Hall, Carl	f	6-12	0-0	4-8	4	7	11	0	16	1	0	3	1	23
02	Armstead, Malcolm	g	2-5	1-3	0-0	0	2	2	3	5	2	0	0	0	22
03	Wessel, Evan	g	3-6	2-4	0-0	1	2	3	2	8	4	0	0	0	22
31	Baker, Ron	g	3-7	2-5	0-0	2	1	3	0	8	5	1	0	4	21
00	Lufile, Chadrack		3-4	0-0	0-1	0	3	3	0	6	0	1	0	0	14
05	Williams, Demetric		2-3	0-0	3-4	0	0	0	4	7	3	3	0	0	20
15	Wiggins, Nick		2-2	0-0	0-0	0	0	0	0	4	0	0	0	0	5
23	VanVleet, Fred		4-6	1-1	0-0	1	3	4	1	9	5	1	0	4	17
32	Cotton, Tekele		3-6	0-1	2-5	2	5	7	2	8	2	2	0	0	21
50	White, Jake		1-1	0-0	0-0	0	3	3	0	2	0	0	0	2	9
	Team					0	1	1							
	Totals		35-67	7-19	9-18	13	28	41	15	86	23	8	3	12	200

FG % 1st Half: 16-32 50.0% 2nd half: 19-35 54.3% Game: 35-67 52.2%
3FG % 1st Half: 4-12 33.3% 2nd half: 3-7 42.9% Game: 7-19 36.8%
FT % 1st Half: 2-4 50.0% 2nd half: 7-14 50.0% Game: 9-18 50.0%

Deadball Rebounds 2

Officials: Joe DeRosa, Bert Smith, Terry Oglesby
Technical fouls: Tulsa-None. Wichita State-None.
Attendance: 10389

Score by periods	1st	2nd	Total
Tulsa	27	33	60
Wichita State	38	48	86

WSU's Malcolm Armstead brings the ball up court against Tulsa's Rashad Ray in the second half at Koch Arena.
By Fernando Salazar, Wichita Eagle

WICHITA STATE 59
SOUTHERN MISS 51

RUNNING ON BELIEF
SHORTHANDED WSU OVERCOMES 12-POINT HOLE AT INTRUST

BY PAUL SUELLENTROP

Wichita State keeps losing players and winning games. It doesn't make much sense, and it doesn't need to. The Shockers are 11-1 and can enjoy Christmas break with great satisfaction.

If coach Gregg Marshall needed to convince the guys in his locker room they could win short-handed, he did a marvelous job. Any non-believers are clearly converts after Saturday's 59-51 win over Southern Mississippi in front of 9,691 fans at Intrust Bank Arena.

"I don't think there's any doubters in there now," WSU coach Gregg Marshall said. "We're down another guy. We go from nine to eight. They stepped up. It's an amazing group."

Right: WSU's Malcolm Armstead shoots for three against Southern Mississippi in the first half at Intrust Bank Arena.
By Fernando Salazar, Wichita Eagle

Facing Page: WSU's Demetric Williams drives to the basket against Southern Mississippi's Dwayne Davis in the second half.
By Fernando Salazar, Wichita Eagle

WSU's Tekele Cotton (32) fights for a loose ball with Southern Mississippi's Dwayne Davis.
By Fernando Salazar, Wichita Eagle

WSU, already missing three injured start-ers, lost reserve forward Jake White to back spasms minutes before the game. He left warm-ups and later returned, in uniform, to watch from the bench.

That left eight healthy players and the Shockers needed every one of them to fight off physical, yet small, Southern Mississippi (8-4). WSU trailed 28-17 after a miserable offensive first half and trailed by 12 early in the second half. After Southern Miss responded to one rally with its own burst, the Shockers trailed 47-40 with 8:01 to play.

Seven points looked closer to 70 in a game with lots of defense and no style points.

WSU, however, disregarded the first 30 minutes and found ways to beat the press and the zone defense. It outscored the Eagles 19-4 in the final 8:01 and 10-0 in the final 3:22 after

trailing 51-49.

"Energy got us going," WSU guard Mal-colm Armstead said. "We locked in a little more defensively. A couple players made shots and it gave us a little more energy."

In a game that should be celebrated for defense, the offensive highlights will stand out. Demetric Williams led WSU with 17 points. Nick Wiggins added 12 and Cleanthony Early 11. WSU shot 38 percent in the first half and 50 percent in the second half.

Williams signaled the drama to come with his three from the corner, beating the shot-clock buzzer, to cut the Southern Miss lead to 36-32. He beat the shot clock again, this time with a long two-pointer, to keep WSU within 47-43.

That's when WSU's offense really picked up. The Shockers loosened up Southern Mississippi's defensive grip on the game by throwing over the press for layups and throwing over the zone for open shots and lobs. The Eagles don't play anybody taller than 6-foot-6 and it showed late in the game. WSU grabbed eight offensive rebounds and scored nine second-chance points in the second half, 16 total in the lane.

"We're a very under-sized, inexperienced team," Southern Mississippi coach Donnie Tyndall said. "Our lack of size, especially the second half, their bigs kind of wore us down."

Chadrack Lufile's three-point play gave them a 49-48 lead with 3:44 to play. Wiggins followed in his own miss to tie it 51-all after a Neil Watson three. Then Wiggins struck again, hammering in a high-flying tip dunk for a 53-51 lead.

Wiggins' dunk yanked any reluctant fans to their feet and they likely stayed upright the rest of the way.

"Nick parachuted out of the upper concourse for that dunk," Marshall said.

Then the Shockers put it away at the foul line.

Ehimen Orukpe, after grabbing a rebound, made two foul shots for a 55-51 lead with 41 seconds to play. Early made two more for a 57-51 lead and a layup by Williams wrapped up the victory

WSU held Southern Miss to 18 of 50 shooting (36 percent). Jerrold Brooks led the Golden Eagles with 18 points.

White's absence started the game on a sour note. On the court, WSU's problems started when point guard Malcolm Armstead exited with his second foul with seven minutes to play in the first half. The Shockers managed three points the rest of half, slumping from a 14-all tie to a 28-17 halftime disadvantage.

Southern Miss led 21-15 when a nightmare stretch sunk the Shockers. It started with Williams' turnover, continued through two missed dunks by Early (both on lob passes), a charge by Fred VanVleet (wiping away a basket) and two more turnovers. After Early's second dunk

bounced away, Brooks made a three to give Southern Miss a 26-16 lead and Marshall tore off his jacket.

WSU shot 5 of 22 in the first half, 1 of 8 from three-point range, and committed 13 turnovers. WSU grabbed six offensive rebounds, and didn't score after any of them. Early missed all seven of his shots and no Shocker made more than one. Williams and Nick Wiggins each scored five points.

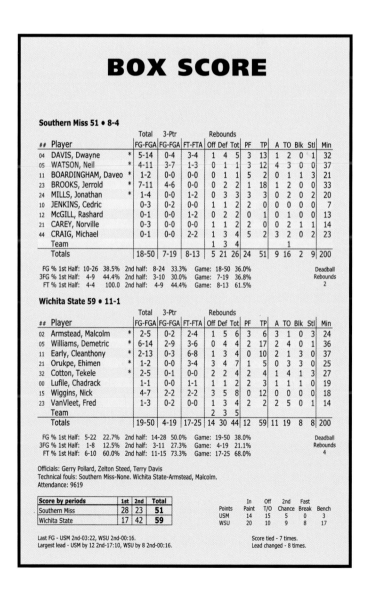

STATEMENT START
SHOCKERS POP UNI IN MVC OPENER

BY PAUL SUELLENTROP

Wichita State hasn't lowered its expectations with three starters injured. Now the Missouri Valley Conference knows why.

The Shockers routed Northern Iowa, picked third in the preseason poll, 66-41 on Sunday at Koch Arena. WSU's defense blanketed UNI's three-point shooters and an efficient offense did the rest in a victory surprising for its ease over an experienced team with a reputation for toughness.

WSU senior Demetric Williams hopes everybody who voted the Shockers fourth in the preseason poll pays attention. And everybody who further dismissed the Shockers (12-1, 1-0 MVC) because of the injury problems.

"We're ready to show everybody we're not fourth in this league," Williams said. "There's still a lot of guys on this team."

All nine of them helped bury the Panthers (7-6, 0-1). Starters Carl Hall, Ron Baker and Evan Wessel

Right: WSU's Cleanthony Early scores a basket in the first period. WSU won 66-41 and Early was the top scorer for both teams finishing with 16 points. *By Jaime Green, Wichita Eagle*

Facing Page: WSU's Ehimen Orukpe dunks the ball in the second period against Northern Iowa. *By Jaime Green, Wichita Eagle*

watched from the bench, but UNI coach Ben Jacobson saw little difference from the team he watched with a full roster.

WSU held the Panthers, who entered the game making 37.1 percent of their three-pointers, to 3-of-17 shooting from behind the arc.

"Their defense and rebounding hasn't changed with what's happened with some of the injuries," Jacobson said.

Cleanthony Early led WSU with 16 points, 11 in the first half. Malcolm Armstead added 14. The Shockers scored 22 points in the lane, mostly using their quickness to shoot layups.

Armstead handed out five assists and disrupted UNI's defense with his drives. WSU made 46 percent of its shots, committed 10 turnovers - second-lowest amount this season - and made 14 of 20 free throws.

No Panther reached double figures. Jake Koch led UNI with seven points on 2-of-8 shooting. Guard Deon Mitchell, UNI's leading scorer at 12.4 points, scored four. Guard Marc Sonnen, making 43.7 percent of his threes, went 0 for 2 and scored two points.

"That was as well as we've played for 40 minutes defensively in some time, and that's the way it's going to have to be," WSU coach Gregg Marshall said.

WSU pulled away slowly in the first half to build a 30-18 lead. Then it decisively won the start of the second half and never allowed the Panthers to make a move.

Ehimen Orukpe started WSU's second-half burst with a dunk. Armstead's three made it 35-19. Then he stripped the ball from Seth Tuttle, leading to a layup for Williams. A jumper by Tekele Cotton extended WSU's lead to 39-19 and the Panthers didn't get closer than 14 the rest of the way.

"We didn't get baskets on our first couple of possessions, and coming out of halftime, I felt like we needed to to get the score under 10," Jacobson said. "We weren't scoring at all. Had we got it under 10, you've got a reasonable chance."

The Shockers, even with the comfy lead at halftime, never wavered. They pushed the lead to 30 late in the game.

Wichita State's Tekele Cotton dribbles against Northern Iowa in the Shockers' Valley opener.
By Jaime Green, Wichita Eagle

"Ehimen got that dunk, and I felt like it took the momentum from them," Williams said. "We didn't have any scoring droughts. We kept our defense the same."

WSU's defense dominated the first half by covering up UNI's shooters and protecting the lane. The Panthers made 1 of 6 threes in the first half and 7of 25 shots.

Armstead set up the offense with his drives to the basket. He fed Early for WSU's first basket and he sliced through the defense for a layup. UNI couldn't stay with Early, either. He scored 11 first-half points, making 5 of 6 shots.

The Shockers built their lead midway through the half with an 11-2 run capped by Early's left-handed layup for a 23-11 lead. After the Panthers closed to within 23-14, Williams sank a long three to start a 7-2 run that pushed the lead to 30-16.

BOX SCORE

UNI 41 • 7-6, 0-1

##	Player		Total FG-FGA	3-Ptr FG-FGA	FT-FTA	Off	Def	Tot	PF	TP	A	TO	Blk	Stl	Min
10	Tuttle, Seth	f	1-2	0-0	1-2	0	2	2	2	3	0	2	0	0	17
20	Koch, Jake	f	2-8	1-3	2-2	1	0	1	2	7	1	1	0	1	22
01	Mitchell, Deon	g	2-5	0-1	0-0	0	2	2	1	4	1	4	0	0	21
23	Sonnen, Marc	g	1-3	0-2	0-0	0	2	2	1	2	0	1	0	0	28
52	James, Anthony	g	2-7	0-1	1-2	0	1	1	1	5	1	0	0	1	24
04	Rank, Chip		2-5	2-5	0-0	0	0	0	1	6	0	0	0	1	14
05	Bohannon, Matt		0-3	0-1	0-0	0	1	1	3	0	0	1	0	0	15
12	Singleton, Marvin		0-1	0-0	2-2	0	0	0	2	2	0	0	0	0	8
14	Buss, Nate		1-5	0-3	0-0	0	0	0	2	2	1	0	1	0	17
21	Morrison, Matt		2-3	0-1	2-2	0	0	0	1	6	3	1	0	0	13
24	Martino, Max		1-1	0-0	0-0	0	2	2	2	2	1	0	0	0	12
33	Pehl, Austin		1-3	0-0	0-0	1	3	4	0	2	1	2	0	0	6
	Team					3	4	7							
	Totals		15-46	3-17	8-10	5	17	22	18	41	9	12	1	3	200

FG % 1st Half: 7-25 28.0% 2nd half: 8-21 38.1% Game: 15-46 32.6%
3FG % 1st Half: 1-6 16.7% 2nd half: 2-11 18.2% Game: 3-17 17.6%
FT % 1st Half: 3-4 75.0% 2nd half: 5-6 83.3% Game: 8-10 80.0%
Deadball Rebounds 1

Wichita State 66 • 12-1, 1-0

##	Player		Total FG-FGA	3-Ptr FG-FGA	FT-FTA	Off	Def	Tot	PF	TP	A	TO	Blk	Stl	Min
11	Early, Cleanthony	f	6-11	1-4	3-4	2	4	6	2	16	1	2	1	2	27
21	Orukpe, Ehimen	c	2-4	0-0	1-2	2	4	6	2	5	0	1	2	0	20
02	Armstead, Malcolm	g	4-6	2-3	4-6	0	4	4	2	14	5	4	0	3	26
05	Williams, Demetric	g	5-8	1-1	1-2	0	4	4	1	12	3	0	0	1	29
32	Cotton, Tekele	g	4-6	1-2	3-4	2	4	6	0	12	0	1	0	1	32
00	Lufile, Chadrack		0-2	0-0	0-0	0	0	0	2	0	0	0	1	1	11
15	Wiggins, Nick		0-3	0-1	0-0	0	0	0	3	0	1	1	0	1	14
23	VanVleet, Fred		1-5	0-1	0-0	0	0	0	1	2	1	0	0	2	19
50	White, Jake		1-5	1-5	2-2	2	6	8	3	5	0	1	0	0	22
	Team					5	1	6							
	Totals		23-50	6-17	14-20	13	27	40	15	66	11	10	4	9	200

FG % 1st Half: 12-25 48.0% 2nd half: 11-25 44.0% Game: 23-50 46.0%
3FG % 1st Half: 3-8 37.5% 2nd half: 3-9 33.3% Game: 6-17 35.3%
FT % 1st Half: 3-6 50.0% 2nd half: 11-14 78.6% Game: 14-20 70.0%
Deadball Rebounds 3

Officials: Mike Stuart, Tom Eades, Mark Whitehead
Technical fouls: UNI-None. Wichita State-None.
Attendance: 10506

Score by periods	1st	2nd	Total
UNI	18	23	41
Wichita State	30	36	66

Points	In Paint	Off T/O	2nd Chance	Fast Break	Bench
UNI	16	10	6	0	20
WSU	22	14	8	6	7

Last FG - UNI 2nd-00:42, WSU 2nd-01:13.
Largest lead - UNI by 3 1st-19:34, WSU by 30 2nd-05:51.

Score tied - 0 times.
Lead changed - 3 times.

EHIMEN ORUKPE

THE QUIET ONE
HUMILITY, DETERMINATION DEFINE ORUKPE

BY PAUL SUELLENTROP

The conversation thread on Shockernet.net is the stuff of legend in the world of Internet fan forums - 3,912 messages dating to 2007. It is a voluminous amount of talk about Wichita State's quietest basketball player, senior Ehimen Orukpe.

"Any news on Orukpe?" the topic begins, and it careens through his on-again, off-again departure from Nigeria, his attempt to get eligible, two seasons at a junior college and three with the Shockers.

Five years and so many cheers.

Fans, inspired by his story, adopted him as a favorite in Koch Arena. His playing time didn't matter. His sometimes-awkward attempts at scoring didn't matter. When Orukpe dunked or blocked a shot, fans cheered his successes with an investment that surpassed wins and losses.

"Sometimes, it's still overwhelming," he said. "They showed me a lot of love. I just look at it as sometimes, when I do something to help our team, they cheer for it."

Orukpe, a 7-foot center from Lagos, Nigeria, is winding down a Shocker career that started when he

The journey to Wichita for Ehimen Orukpe started in 2007 and ended six years later.
By Fernando Salazar, Wichita Eagle

signed in May 2007. He came to the United States a year later and, unable to win approval from the NCAA despite outstanding academic performances, attended Three Rivers (Mo.) Community College. He redshirted one season and played in 2009-10 before returning to WSU. His playing time increased each season as he improved his skills to match his height and athletic ability.

As a senior, he's started 28 games and averaged 2.8 points and 4.5 rebounds. His 54 blocks are tied for sixth on WSU's single-season list.

"Everybody on the team wants the best for him," guard Tekele Cotton said. "He went through a lot to try and get into the school. He's here and he's able to play, and (fans) root for him a lot."

He played his best stretch at a crucial time, helping the Shockers survive an injury to forward Carl Hall that cost him seven games in December and January. In those games, Orukpe averaged 5.7 points, 8.1 rebounds and 3.2 blocks, all while recovering from a sprained ankle that cost him three games.

The height, the story and the academic skills add up to a person who naturally attracts attention. Orukpe stands out in a crowd, even in the classroom. He carries a 3.52 grade-point average in mathematics, with a business minor. He earned a spot on the Missouri Valley Conference Scholar-Athlete team.

"A joy," WSU coach Gregg Marshall said. "Zero maintenance."

Orukpe prefers to work in the background, speak softly and stay humble. Like former teammate Garrett Stutz, also a 7-footer, he often exits the locker room wearing his hood as a barrier against stares.

"He's very shy," said Dominic Okon, WSU's director of operations and a fellow Nigerian. "He doesn't want people to see him as a smart person, or just as a basketball player because of his height."

Don't mistake shyness for aloofness. Orukpe is touched by the fans and may have tried too hard to reward them on the court.

"Everybody in Wichita was invested, and they feel they are a part of his journey," Okon said. "That, in itself, is a burden to him because he always wants to show his appreciation and gets ahead of himself on the court."

His classwork offers a different kind of payback to fans.

His favorite class at WSU was Calculus II. At Three Rivers, he earned an A in American History to 1877 in his first semester in the United States. While his practice schedule kept him from an engineering major, he plans to work in the field after he is done with basketball.

Smart guy, but not one to talk big. Cotton, Orukpe's closest friend on the team, sees that humility often. While he gladly talks to fans, he also gladly lets others take the bulk of the attention.

"He's 7-feet, so if we go somewhere people are going to notice he's on the basketball team," Cotton said. "He really doesn't like to talk about basketball or brag that he's smart. He's humble."

A demanding sports life and a demanding major can be an exhausting combination. His afternoon routine usually includes an hour of weights, video study with the team and around two hours of practice. Evenings are devoted to homework and rest. His studies in Nigeria and his family's emphasis on education prepared him well for class work in college.

"I never wanted to come home with bad grades, because my dad would be mad at me, " he said. "I made good grades and I studied. The more you put into it, the more you get out of it."

Free time is rare. "Anger Management" and "Two And A Half Men" are his favorite TV shows. He plays video games such as Mortal Kombat and Batman. His musical tastes range from reggae to hip-hop.

"I like to play adventure games," he said. "My teammates always make fun of me because I don't play a lot of basketball video games."

With Okon's sons or on rides with Cotton, Orukpe's humor comes out. He plays video games with Okon's sons, Jaden and Jordan, during his frequent visits to their house.

"He's a normal kid," Cotton said. "He's fun to be around. We drive home and we talk about a lot of different things. The stuff he brings up is funny, stuff that happens. He likes to joke."

Orukpe wants to play basketball professionally after college. When that is finished, engineering beckons, following in his father's footsteps. He is prepared to live anywhere, wherever his careers take him.

"Building stuff," he said. "I've been around a lot of construction work, building bridges, factories. I want to be around that."

WICHITA STATE 82
S. ILLINOIS 76

EARLY, AND OFTEN
WSU JUNIOR SCORES 39 IN WIN OVER SIU

BY PAUL SUELLENTROP

I t took a very un-Gregg Marshall like performance for No. 23 Wichita State to survive on Wednesday night. Marshall didn't mind at all after watching forward Cleanthony Early score 39 points in an 82-76 win over Southern Illinois at Koch Arena.

"That's a big-time number," Marshall, WSU's coach, said. "He makes it look easy."

Nothing about WSU's win came easy, regardless of how effortless it appeared Early poured in his season high. He made 13 of 19 shots, 5 of 9 three-pointers, and finished with the most points by a Shocker since Xavier McDaniel scored 44 against West Texas State in 1985. It is the highest total by a Missouri Valley Conference player this season and tied for fifth nationally.

SIU (7-8, 0-4 MVC) battled the Shockers (15-1, 4-0) all the way, leading 43-34 at halftime and rallying from a 10-point deficit in the second half

Right: WSU's Demetric Williams goes up for two against Southern Illinois' Jeff Early.
By Fernando Salazar, Wichita Eagle

Facing Page: WSU's Tekele Cotton drives the ball up court against Southern Illinois' Jeff Early.
By Fernando Salazar, Wichita Eagle

to make it close in the final minute. With starting center Dantiel Daniels out with a sprained ankle, the Salukis often played a lineup with no player taller than 6-foot-5.

"It was definitely the height advantage and just knowing how to use your body against a smaller defender," Early said. "They gave me a couple open perimeter shots and I just found a way to get it going."

Marshall's teams are defined by balanced scoring, balanced minutes and superb defense. Not Wednesday. SIU's changing defenses took the Shockers out of their comfort zone and they didn't play with their customary energy on defense in the first half.

Early is talented enough to cover up a lot of issues. He out-dueled SIU's Desmar Jackson, who scored 28 points.

Early, a 6-foot-8 junior, played 36 minutes and was one of two Shockers to reach double figures. He scored WSU's first seven points on his way to 16 in the first half. He scored eight of WSU's first 13 points to start the second half, giving WSU a 44-43 lead with a three-point play. When SIU made its final push, cutting the lead to 73-69, Early made a three and a layup to give the Shockers a 78-71 advantage.

"That No. 11 is pretty good," SIU coach Barry Hinson said. "Gosh, was he good."

With Early waking up the memories of McDaniel and other great scorers, center Ehimen Orukpe did the same for defense. He blocked seven shots, most by a Shocker since Antoine Carr swatted seven against West Texas State in 1981.

"Coach (Marshall) calls him an eraser," WSU guard Tekele Cotton said. "He's there to clean it up."

SIU's zone defense frustrated the Shockers in the first half. They committed nine turnovers, twice throwing the ball directly to a defender, that led to 17 SIU points. SIU, meanwhile, made shots from all angles and stunned the crowd with a half-time lead.

The Shockers expected harsh words from Marshall at halftime.

"We felt it ourselves," Early said. "We knew were playing down to our competition. We felt like we had to step it up."

WSU, playing harder on defense, led 57-50 with 14:12 to play and 70-60 with 7:02 remaining.

It wasn't enough to shake SIU. WSU committed two turnovers in the final minute and SIU cut the lead to 78-76. WSU's Malcolm Armstead made two free throws and then stole the ball from SIU's Anthony Beane. Two more free throws from Armstead with 15 seconds to play ended the drama.

WSU's Cleanthony Early goes up for two against Southern Illinois' Davante Drinkard in the second half at Koch Arena.
By Fernando Salazar, Wichita Eagle

BOX SCORE

Southern Illinois 76 • 7-8, 0-4

##	Player		Total FG-FGA	3-Ptr FG-FGA	FT-FTA	Off	Def	Tot	PF	TP	A	TO	Blk	Stl	Min
02	Kendal Brown-Surles	*	3-5	3-4	0-0	0	0	0	3	9	2	2	0	1	28
03	Desmar Jackson	*	10-19	3-9	5-7	1	4	5	3	28	0	1	0	1	35
04	Davante Drinkard	*	0-4	0-0	0-0	2	1	3	1	0	0	1	1	0	25
22	Jeff Early	*	6-9	0-0	1-1	0	5	5	5	13	2	3	0	1	24
25	Anthony Beane	*	5-12	2-3	2-2	0	0	0	3	14	3	2	0	2	35
01	Jalen Pendleton		2-2	0-0	0-0	1	2	3	4	4	0	1	0	1	16
12	T.J. Lindsay		0-0	0-0	0-0	0	0	0	0	0	0	0	0	0	9
21	Josh Swan		1-6	0-0	6-6	2	4	6	1	8	2	0	0	1	28
	Team					2	4	6							
	Totals		27-57	8-16	14-16	8	20	28	20	76	9	10	1	7	200

FG % 1st Half: 17-32 53.1%   2nd half: 10-25 40.0%   Game: 27-57 47.4%   Deadball
3FG % 1st Half: 4-7 57.1%   2nd half: 4-9 44.4%   Game: 8-16 50.0%   Rebounds
FT % 1st Half: 5-5 100.0%   2nd half: 9-11 81.8%   Game: 14-16 87.5%   0

Wichita State 82 • 15-1, 4-0

##	Player		Total FG-FGA	3-Ptr FG-FGA	FT-FTA	Off	Def	Tot	PF	TP	A	TO	Blk	Stl	Min
02	Armstead, Malcolm	*	2-7	1-3	4-4	1	3	4	3	9	9	2	0	2	33
05	Williams, Demetric	*	1-5	1-4	1-2	0	1	1	4	4	1	1	0	1	26
11	Early, Cleanthony	*	13-19	5-9	8-10	3	3	6	2	39	0	3	2	1	36
21	Orukpe, Ehimen	*	5-7	0-0	0-2	3	6	9	4	10	0	2	7	0	27
32	Cotton, Tekele	*	2-3	0-0	5-8	2	2	4	2	9	6	1	1	1	23
00	Lufile, Chadrack		1-3	0-0	1-2	1	0	1	0	3	0	0	0	0	9
15	Wiggins, Nick		1-4	1-3	1-2	0	2	2	1	4	0	2	1	0	25
23	VanVleet, Fred		1-3	0-1	0-0	0	3	3	1	2	4	0	0	1	14
50	White, Jake		1-1	0-0	0-0	0	3	3	0	2	0	2	0	0	7
	Team					3	1	4							
	Totals		27-52	8-20	20-30	13	24	37	17	82	20	13	11	6	200

FG % 1st Half: 12-25 48.0%   2nd half: 15-27 55.6%   Game: 27-52 51.9%   Deadball
3FG % 1st Half: 3-9 33.3%   2nd half: 5-11 45.5%   Game: 8-20 40.0%   Rebounds
FT % 1st Half: 7-10 70.0%   2nd half: 13-20 65.0%   Game: 20-30 66.7%   2

Officials: Mark Schnur, Jeff Campbell, Brad Ferrie
Technical fouls: Southern Illinois-None. Wichita State-None.
Attendance: 10306

Score by periods	1st	2nd	Total
Southern Illinois	43	33	76
Wichita State	34	48	82

	Points	In Paint	Off T/O	2nd Chance	Fast Break	Bench
SIU		28	23	15	4	12
WSU		34	16	16	2	11

Last FG - SIU 2nd-01:20, WSU 2nd-02:26.
Largest lead - SIU by 11 1st-04:17, WSU by 10 2nd-07:02.

Score tied - 7 times.
Lead changed - 10 times.

WICHITA STATE 67
CREIGHTON 64

INSIDE ADDITION
WSU'S WORK ON OFFENSIVE GLASS GOOD FOR VICTORY OVER CREIGHTON

BY PAUL SUELLENTROP

Wichita State made the best of 44 missed shots and its reward is a share of first place in the Missouri Valley Conference.

Nobody recommends that strategy, but it works with a team of ferocious rebounders. The Shockers - no surprise to No. 12 Creighton - are that and more and they slipped past the Bluejays 67-64 on Saturday at packed and blacked-out Koch Arena.

"They killed us on the boards," Creighton forward Doug McDermott said. "It seemed like we couldn't get any rebounds."

That is becoming the theme of these matchups.

The Shockers out-rebounded Creighton in both games last season and their edge in quickness and strength showed again on Saturday. Wichita State grabbed 22 offensive rebounds and scored 23 second-chance points.

With that effort, the Shockers survived bad shooting from the field and the line. They missed 19 of 23 three-pointers and 10 of 19 foul shots.

"The defense and rebounding was just good

Creighton's Gregory Echenique, bottom, fights for a rebound during the first half against Wichita State's Ehimen Orukpe.
By Travis Heying, The Wichita Eagle

Wichita State's Carl Hall, right, fights for a rebound against Creighton's Grant Gibbs.
By Fernando Salazar, The Wichita Eagle

enough," WSU coach Gregg Marshall said. "Not too many teams can hold Creighton to 64."

The Shockers (17-2, 6-1 MVC) snapped Creighton's 11-game win streak and moved into a tie with the Bluejays (17-2, 6-1).

"Our problems started when the ball went up to the rim," Creighton coach Greg McDermott said. "To come in here and win, you've got to have a little more toughness."

Shocker toughness is rarely questioned and Saturday showed why. Carl Hall, in his second game back after missing seven with a broken right thumb, scored 17 points and grabbed 13 rebounds, six offensive. Guard Tekele Cotton had a career-high eight rebounds. Guard Malcolm Armstead grabbed six.

"They have trouble ... rebounding, and we try to take advantage of that with our size," Hall said.

Doug McDermott led Creighton with 25 points, his high in five meetings with WSU. He made 10 of 19 shots. The Shockers kept him off the line - 1 of 2 - and made him work for his shots. Cotton, Hall and Cleanthony Early took turns guarding him.

"They're great offensively," Cotton said. "I just tried to do my part and limit his easy touches and good looks at the goal."

WSU's poor shooting almost cost it the game. The Shockers couldn't build on their lead because of offensive droughts. Hall missed 5 of 6 free throws in the final two minutes.

They rarely turned the ball over - seven times,

Wichita State's Carl Hall takes a shot over Creighton's Ethan Wragge during the second half.
By Travis Heying, The Wichita Eagle

three in the second half - and they turned all those possessions into 71 shots, 16 more than Creighton.

Armstead came up with two of the game's big-gest sequences in the final minutes. With WSU up 64-63, he stole the ball from Doug McDermott. The teams traded a free throw each, then Armstead made two foul shots with 15.2 seconds to play for the final margin.

Creighton's Ethan Wragge missed a three from the corner - on an inbound play - with eight seconds remaining. After two misses by Hall, Wragge missed again from around 24 feet at the top of the key before the buzzer.

"We got we wanted," Greg McDermott said. "We got him two good looks in the last few seconds to tie it. The game was decided long before those shots. You can't turn it over twice as many times as they do and give them that many second opportunities on the backboards and expect to be in the game. And yet, we still had a chance to tie it."

Marshall wanted to foul on Creighton's final possession, which started with 7.1 seconds to play.

He saw no sense in giving the nation's top three-point shooting team (45.4 percent) a chance to tie.

"We tried to do it," Marshall said. "There's a fine line between fouling and trying to foul too hard. Malcolm was the guy that tried to foul, and they didn't call it."

The win puts WSU in position to finish the first half of MVC play in great position. The Shockers survived injuries. They bounced back from a loss at Evansville. They beat the preseason favorite to hold serve at home. They play two of their next three at Koch Arena.

"We didn't allow them to separate," Marshall said. "They're a very good team and they've got a great chance to be right there at the end. Hopefully, we can be right there with them."

Wichita State's Carl Hall grabs a rebound and is fouled with less than a minute to play. .
By Travis Heying, The Wichita Eagle

BOX SCORE

Creighton 64 • 17-2, 6-1

##	Player		Total FG-FGA	3-Ptr FG-FGA	FT-FTA	Off	Def	Tot	PF	TP	A	TO	Blk	Stl	Min
03	McDermott, Doug	f	10-19	4-5	1-2	2	4	6	2	25	1	2	0	1	35
00	Echenique, Gregory	c	3-5	0-0	3-7	6	7	13	1	9	0	2	5	0	29
01	Chatman, Austin	g	3-9	1-3	2-2	1	5	6	2	9	2	4	0	1	38
10	Gibbs, Grant	g	5-9	1-2	3-4	1	4	5	5	14	8	4	0	1	39
12	Manigat, Jahenns	g	0-4	0-2	0-0	1	0	1	5	0	1	0	0	0	13
02	Stormberg, Taylor		0-0	0-0	0-0	0	1	1	0	0	0	0	0	0	2
22	Dingman, Avery		1-3	1-2	1-2	1	2	3	0	4	1	0	0	0	22
24	Johnson, Nevin		0-0	0-0	0-0	0	0	0	0	0	0	2	0	0	6
34	Wragge, Ethan		1-6	1-6	0-0	0	2	2	1	3	0	0	1	0	16
	Team					1	3	4							
	Totals		23-55	8-20	10-17	13	28	41	16	64	13	14	6	3	200

FG % 1st Half: 11-26 42.3% 2nd half: 12-29 41.4% Game: 23-55 41.8%
3FG % 1st Half: 4-7 57.1% 2nd half: 4-13 30.8% Game: 8-20 40.0%
FT % 1st Half: 7-13 53.8% 2nd half: 3-4 75.0% Game: 10-17 58.8%

Deadball Rebounds 4

Wichita State 67 • 17-2, 6-1

##	Player		Total FG-FGA	3-Ptr FG-FGA	FT-FTA	Off	Def	Tot	PF	TP	A	TO	Blk	Stl	Min
02	Armstead, Malcolm	*	5-14	2-8	3-3	2	4	6	0	15	5	2	0	2	36
05	Williams, Demetric	*	5-11	0-4	0-2	1	0	1	1	10	3	1	0	1	31
11	Early, Cleanthony	*	5-10	1-4	2-4	0	0	0	2	13	1	1	0	1	28
21	Orukpe, Ehimen	*	1-1	0-0	0-0	1	3	4	3	2	0	0	2	0	13
32	Cotton, Tekele	*	0-10	0-2	3-4	3	5	8	3	3	1	1	0	1	32
00	Lufile, Chadrack		0-0	0-0	0-0	0	0	0	2	0	0	0	0	0	3
15	Wiggins, Nick		1-5	1-3	0-0	0	0	0	1	3	0	1	0	0	11
22	Hall, Carl		8-15	0-0	1-6	6	7	13	3	17	0	0	1	0	25
23	VanVleet, Fred		0-2	0-1	0-0	0	2	2	1	0	2	0	1	0	10
50	White, Jake		2-3	0-1	0-0	2	1	3	0	4	0	0	0	0	11
	Team					7	0	7				1			
	Totals		27-71	4-23	9-19	22	22	44	16	67	12	7	4	5	200

FG % 1st Half: 15-40 37.5% 2nd half: 12-31 38.7% Game: 27-71 38.0%
3FG % 1st Half: 3-15 20.0% 2nd half: 1-8 12.5% Game: 4-23 17.4%
FT % 1st Half: 3-6 50.0% 2nd half: 6-13 46.2% Game: 9-19 47.4%

Deadball Rebounds 4

Officials: Scott Thornley, Tom Eades, Don Daily
Technical fouls: Creighton-None. Wichita State-None.
Attendance: 10506
Creighton ranked 10th by USA Today coaches and 12th by AP
Creighton's 11-game win streak snapped.

Score by periods	1st	2nd	Total
Creighton	33	31	64
Wichita State	36	31	67

	Points	In Paint	Off T/O	2nd Chance	Fast Break	Bench
CU		20	6	5	0	7
WSU		44	11	23	2	24

S. ILLINOIS 68
WICHITA STATE 64

WSU LOSES AGAIN
LAST-PLACE SOUTHERN ILLINOIS HANDS SHOCKERS THIRD STRAIGHT DEFEAT

BY PAUL SUELLENTROP

CARBONDALE, Ill. -- Long scoring droughts. Opponents celebrating wildly. Opponents making the winning plays. These scenes are becoming painfully familiar for Wichita State, which lost its third game in a row on Tuesday. This one is hard to explain.

Last-place Southern Illinois upset the Shockers 64-62 at SIU Arena, moving the panic-meter from slump to collapse for a team ranked No. 15 nationally not too long ago. SIU ended a six-game losing streak by breaking 60 points for the first time since Jan. 15.

SIU Arena, where WSU had won three straight, seemed the perfect spot for the Shockers to get well after losses to Indiana State and Northern Iowa. Instead, the Shockers, ranked No. 22 in the coaches poll, are desperately searching for answers and falling out of the Missouri Valley Conference race.

"We'll have to try to regroup, somehow," WSU coach Gregg Marshall said. "We really played well, got up 14 or 15. Then we stopped guarding at

Wichita State's Jake White latches onto a rebound during the second half against SIU in Carbondale.
By Aaron Eisenhauer, The Southern

Wichita State's Carl Hall looks to pass the ball during the first half against SIU. *By Aaron Eisenhauer, The Southern*

the end of the first half."

The Shockers (19-5, 8-4 MVC) departed angry about a no-call and a goaltending call on Ehimen Orukpe that gave SIU (9-14, 2-10) the winning basket with two seconds to play. SIU guard Jalen Pendleton bulled his way into the lane, knocking over WSU's Demetric Williams, before lofting a shot from about 10 feet. Orukpe blocked it and the officials called goaltending to break the 62-all tie.

"I was going to go for (the block) earlier, but I tried to wait for the charge, to see if they were going to call the charge, before I blocked it," Orukpe said. "I think I hit before its peak."

So did Marshall, who pegged the sarcasm meter with his assessment.

"I thought it was a great call," he said.

WSU's Carl Hall missed a desperation shot at the buzzer, while Marshall tried to call time-out. SIU fans didn't storm the court, as Northern Iowa's did on Saturday. They did celebrate loudly and coach Barry Hinson hugged players at mid-court, pumped his fist at the fans and charged into the student section to share his biggest victory in a trying season.

"The best feeling is walking off that floor and seeing our fans and seeing how excited they were, and walking in that locker room and seeing those kids jump around," Hinson said. "We just had a good week of therapy."

Demetric Williams led WSU with 15 points

Southern Illinois players ask and receive a goaltending call against WSU's Ehimen Orukpe, giving SIU a two-point lead with two seconds remaining. *By Aaron Eisenhauer, The Southern*

and Tekele Cotton added 10 off the bench. The Shockers shot 46.8 percent from the floor and made 8 of 16 three-pointers, ending a two-game shooting slump. Cleanthony Early, who scored 39 points in a win over SIU last month, scored seven and played only 21 minutes, again limited by fouls. Turnovers, as they did against Northern Iowa, hurt. WSU committed 14, leading to 16 SIU points.

Guard T.J. Lindsay led the Salukis with 14 points. The Shockers held SIU to 42 percent shooting. The Salukis compensated by outscoring them 12-3 at the line in the second half and 15-10 for the game.

"We had a little defensive breakdown, but for

the most part I felt the guys in that locker room played hard," Williams said.

While the Shockers didn't get a friendly whistle late, they will soon realize it didn't need to come to that. They led 33-17 in the first half and nodded off, giving SIU life by giving up an 18-3 run. They led 60-58 and had the ball before turning it over on a shot-clock violation. They led 62-60 and allowed Pendleton, a freshman backup who hadn't scored in the past two games, to drive the lane and score with a spin move to tie it 62-all.

Pendleton finished off the Shockers with SIU's final six points, making plays when the Shockers didn't.

"He probably doesn't know any better and

Wichita State head coach Gregg Marshall reacts to a call from the referees during their loss at SIU Arena in Carbondale. *By Aaron Eisenhauer, The Southern*

that's probably to his benefit in that game," Hinson said. "Just go do what you do, son. We put Jalen in to make a defensive play, and sure enough he did and got us points."

WSU is used to being the team that makes those plays. It is used to going on the road and quieting crowds. Now, the Shockers don't seem to know what to do next.

"At the end of the day, we've got to find a way to win," guard Tekele Cotton said. "It's a mental thing and it's a physical thing. We've got to come together, we've got to gel. We've got to be brothers."

WSU solved all its problems in the first 15 minutes of the first half. Then new ones popped up.

With Hall back in the starting lineup and Nick Wiggins debuting, the Shockers hit high gear offensively against the MVC's worst defensive team. They broke out to an 11-4 lead by making their first four shots and kept going. Cotton hit back-to-back threes to make it 23-12, part of a 16-0 run capped by Jake White's layup for a 29-12 lead. Wiggins made two free throws with 5:33 remaining to give the Shockers a 33-17 lead.

All seemed right for WSU.

SIU cut the lead to 33-22 and then WSU turned the ball over on four of five possessions, one an offensive foul on Hall. SIU took advantage with a 14-0 run, fueled by eight points by T.J. Lindsay. WSU's drought continued until Hall made a free throw with 1:22 to play. Wiggins made two more foul shots with 47.1 remaining. The Shockers, who made 12 of 20 shots in the half, didn't make a field goal in the final 5:57.

SIU ended the half on a 18-3 run to trail 36-35 at halftime.

"If (Lindsay) doesn't get going in the first half, we're not in the ballgame," Hinson said.

BOX SCORE

Wichita State 62 • 19-5, 8-4 MVC

##	Player		Total FG-FGA	3-Ptr FG-FGA	FT-FTA	Off	Def	Tot	PF	TP	A	TO	Blk	Stl	Min
11	Early, Cleanthony	f	3-9	0-2	1-1	0	3	3	3	7	0	2	0	0	21
22	Hall, Carl	f	3-6	0-1	2-3	2	3	5	4	8	0	2	3	0	25
02	Armstead, Malcolm	g	2-8	2-4	0-0	0	3	3	3	6	6	4	0	0	33
05	Williams, Demetric	g	5-9	3-4	2-2	0	7	7	2	15	2	1	0	1	35
15	Wiggins, Nick	g	1-3	1-2	4-4	0	4	4	2	7	0	1	0	0	26
00	Lufile, Chadrack		0-0	0-0	0-0	0	0	0	1	0	0	0	0	0	5
21	Orukpe, Fhimen		0-0	0-0	0-0	1	2	3	1	0	0	0	0	0	8
23	VanVleet, Fred		2-5	0-0	0-0	0	1	1	0	4	2	1	0	0	13
32	Cotton, Tekele		4-5	2-3	0-1	1	2	3	3	10	0	2	0	0	20
50	White, Jake		2-2	0-0	1-2	0	1	1	2	5	0	0	0	0	14
	Team					0	3	3				1			
	Totals		22-47	8-16	10-13	4	29	33	21	62	10	14	3	1	200

FG % 1st Half: 12-20 60.0% 2nd half: 10-27 37.0% Game: 22-47 46.8%
3FG % 1st Half: 5-7 71.4% 2nd half: 3-9 33.3% Game: 8-16 50.0%
FT % 1st Half: 7-10 70.0% 2nd half: 3-3 100.0 Game: 10-13 76.9%

Deadball Rebounds 2

Southern Illinois 64 • 9-14, 2-10 MVC

##	Player		Total FG-FGA	3-Ptr FG-FGA	FT-FTA	Off	Def	Tot	PF	TP	A	TO	Blk	Stl	Min
15	Dantiel Daniels	f	0-0	0-0	1-2	0	0	0	2	1	1	0	0	1	9
02	Kendal Brown-Surles	g	2-7	2-5	0-0	0	3	3	0	6	1	0	0	0	29
03	Desmar Jackson	g	5-14	1-4	0-0	0	1	1	3	11	1	2	0	1	32
22	Jeff Early	g	4-9	0-0	3-4	3	4	7	2	11	0	0	0	1	26
25	Anthony Beane, Jr.	g	1-6	0-0	6-8	0	4	4	1	8	1	1	1	0	24
01	Jalen Pendleton		3-4	0-1	2-2	0	2	2	0	8	2	0	0	2	12
04	Davante Drinkard		1-3	0-0	2-2	0	3	3	3	4	0	0	1	0	29
11	Colby Long		0-0	0-0	0-0	0	0	0	0	0	0	0	0	0	4
12	T.J. Lindsay		5-7	4-6	0-0	0	2	2	2	14	2	0	0	0	19
21	Josh Swan		0-0	0-0	1-3	0	1	1	1	1	0	3	0	0	16
	Team					2	2	4							
	Totals		21-50	7-16	15-21	5	22	27	14	64	8	6	2	5	200

FG % 1st Half: 13-29 44.8% 2nd half: 8-21 38.1% Game: 21-50 42.0%
3FG % 1st Half: 6-10 60.0% 2nd half: 1-6 16.7% Game: 7-16 43.8%
FT % 1st Half: 3-4 75.0% 2nd half: 12-17 70.6% Game: 15-21 71.4%

Deadball Rebounds 1

Officials: John Higgins, Mike Stuart, Rick Randall
Technical fouls: Wichita State-None. Southern Illinois-None.
Attendance: 4852

Score by periods	1st	2nd	Total
Wichita State	36	26	62
Southern Illinois	35	29	64

	Points	In Paint	Off T/O	2nd Chance	Fast Break	Bench
	WSU	24	3	5	8	19
	SIU	24	16	4	7	27

Last FG - WSU 2nd-01:07, SIU 2nd-00:02.
Largest lead - WSU by 17 1st-07:28, SIU by 9 2nd-05:45.

Score tied - 3 times.
Lead changed - 3 times.

MALCOLM ARMSTEAD

BELIEVE AND DELIVER
ARMSTEAD NEVER GAVE UP ON BIG DREAMS FOR WICHITA STATE

BY PAUL SUELLENTROP

After beating Pittsburgh, Wichita State associate head coach Chris Jans told Malcolm Armstead to get him to Los Angeles, past No. 1 Gonzaga, for the NCAA's Sweet 16. Armstead wanted Jans to think bigger.

"He looked at me and he said, 'L.A.? We're going to Atlanta,'" Jans said. "It gave me chill bumps. At that point, I thought, 'They believe.'"

Armstead will tell you he believed all the way back in the summer. He saw last season's team win the Missouri Valley Conference title and lose in the first round of the NCAA Tournament. He looked at the players coming back, and the newcomers, and started telling teammates to think Final Four. No matter that WSU last went to the Final Four in 1965 and hadn't been close since 1981.

"The sky is the limit for him, no matter what, and he's always going to be optimistic," freshman Fred VanVleet said. "It's all coming true."

Armstead, a 6-foot senior guard, is playing a large role in making it come true. He earned Most Outstanding Player honors in the West Regional and averages a team-leading 15.5 points - despite below-average shooting - 5.3 rebounds, 3.8 assists and two steals in four NCAA games.

"I came in June ... and he brought (the Final Four) up and told us to be more focused in practice and what-

ever coaches say, just do, because it's for the better of the team," junior Chadrack Lufile said. "He's a senior. Hearing things like that from him really motivated us to be more attentive to coach and more attentive to what's going on."

Understand that Armstead is one of WSU's chattiest players. Even if his teammates leaned toward skepticism in the summer, they remember the talk.

"Whether you're listening or not, he's going to talk," VanVleet said. "Nobody was arguing with him about it, but it was like 'OK, that's Malcolm.' He could talk about anything."

Armstead is getting that chance during the tournament. His play and his story make him irresistible.

On the court, he leads WSU's offense and frustrates defenders with his quirky, left-handed drives and his pop-up three-pointers. When La Salle threatened the Shockers in the Sweet 16 game, Armstead's nine-point response kept them in control.

His story of coming to WSU gets even more attention. He transferred after two seasons at Oregon, a move he calls a business decision, and reunited at WSU with assistant coach Greg Heiar, who coached him at Chipola (Fla.) College for one season.

"Like coaches leave programs for business, for a better situation, I left for a better situation," he said. "Nothing against (Oregon coach Dana Altman). He's a

Wichita State Shockers guard Malcolm Armstead drives past Ohio State Buckeyes forward Deshaun Thomas in the NCAA Tournament regional final at Staples Center in Los Angeles. *By Jaime Green, Wichita Eagle*

great coach. I still talk to him."

WSU didn't have a scholarship, so he took out loans and worked at Lubbers Auto Group in Cheney as a runner. He is counting on professional basketball to pay off the loans. Working at Lubbers paid off in other ways. He drove cars from lot to lot, and washed and detailed them.

"I learned how to balance tires, rotate tires, oil changes, " he said. "I never knew any of that."

Armstead practiced with the Shockers, sometimes missing sessions when work demanded it. From his experience that season, he grew confident the 2012-13 Shockers could do big things. As a senior - one of the few Shockers with significant NCAA Division I experience - he wanted to make sure his teammates knew. He came to WSU desperately wanting to taste the NCAA Tournament for the first time.

"You got to dream it and then you go out and make it happen," he said. "Seeing this group, and knowing my ability, and working as hard as I did and seeing

other players work as hard as they did, it helped us out believing."

Armstead is not the only senior who made high expectations a standard over the summer. Guard Demetric Williams, WSU's lone four-year senior, remembers talking with Carl Hall about their mark on the program.

The 2012 seniors - Toure Murry, David Kyles, Garrett Stutz, Ben Smith and Joe Ragland - won the MVC title and returned the Shockers to the Big Dance for the first time since 2006. The 2012 Shockers, who lost to VCU in the second round, combined good defense with one of the nation's most efficient offenses.

Williams, Hall and Ehimen Orukpe - all seniors - wanted to use defense as their trademark.

"I felt like our legacy could be even more," Williams said. "So we've got to put in the work, we've got to focus real hard and get everybody on the same page. Use our athleticism and our quickness and our defense that we focus on and apply it to this team even more."

WICHITA STATE 68
ILLINOIS STATE 67

WSU RALLIES FOR WIN
SHOCKERS DOWN SEVEN WITH JUST 40 SECONDS LEFT

BY PAUL SUELLENTROP

NORMAL, Ill. -- Teams working to win a conference title often need at least one miracle finish to come out on top. If so, Wichita State's improbable ending arrived in its favor on Sunday with a 68-67 win over Illinois State at Redbird Arena. Cleanthony Early's three-pointer with 5.2 seconds to play provided the winning basket, capping an 8-0 run that started with Early's free throws after a flagrant foul.

The Shockers trailed by seven points with 40 seconds remaining, enough time for them to make every play, rip out the hearts from the home team and celebrate madly on the court.

"We had hope the whole time," WSU guard Malcolm Armstead said. "We never felt down. If we felt that way, we wouldn't have come out with this win."

WSU (22-5, 11-4 Missouri Valley Conference) retains a one-game lead in the MVC over Creighton with three to play. The Shockers are that close to winning back-to-back Valley titles for the first time since 1964 and 1965.

Illinois State (16-11, 8-7) controlled the first half with its defense and scored with ease for much of the second half. Throughout, the Red-

birds set up shop at the foul line and outscored WSU by 20 points on free throws. However, they failed to deliver a knockout blow.

The Redbirds appeared as if they would survive WSU's final rally when center Jackie Carmichael rebounded to protect a 65-60 lead with 51 seconds to play. Carmichael, a Manhattan native, got the ball to Johnny Hill, who drew a foul.

Instead, that play started the unraveling.

Fans started to celebrate what looked like the clincher. Then they noticed the referees huddling at the scorer's table and looking at TV monitor. Carmichael kicked WSU's Tekele Cotton when he grabbed the rebound and, after a video review, received a flagrant foul. Hill made two free throws with 40 seconds to play. Early made two free throws and WSU got the ball, down 67-62 with 40 seconds remaining.

At first, referees didn't call a foul. Then WSU coach Gregg Marshall asked referee Paul Janssen to look at the play. After a review, they hit Carmi-

WSU's Demetric Williams blocks the shot of Illinois State's Tyler Brown.
By Lori Ann Cook-Neisler, The Pantagraph

chael with the foul.

"I didn't know, really, what it was, but I knew there was a kick," Marshall said. "He's coming out of the air, and Cotton's there, and the foot goes to the face area. I'm glad they made the call."

Illinois State coach Dan Muller searched his memory for a precedent and came up empty.

"Never in my entire life," he said. "And I'd be surprised if I see another one. They said he intentionally kicked him above the neck. How Jackie was getting a rebound and intentionally kicking a moving target, I'm not sure."

WSU's Demetric Williams made a three-pointer from the corner to cut the lead to 67-65 with 28 seconds to play. The Shockers pressed and Hill, trying to escape a trap in the corner by dribbling around Carl Hall, fumbled the ball out of bounds with 24 seconds to play.

WSU worked for a shot for nine seconds, leading Marshall to call timeout. Early got free for a three-pointer over Bryant Allen, after the Redbirds switched on defense, to grab the 68-67 lead with 5.2 seconds remaining.

"Just a screen and roll," Early said. "I thought I had the opportunity and I was open for a second."

Armstead, who led WSU with 18 points, found Early with an eight-inch height advantage over Allen.

"I made the read and Cleanthony made the shot," he said. "They switched it and I saw a smaller guy was on Cleanthony."

The Redbirds got the ball to Carmichael near half court. He dribbled past Ehimen Orukpe and got into the lane to shoot a runner that bounced away.

"It's nice to get out of here with a win," Marshall said. "What I commended the guys for was

how they executed down the stretch. They didn't force anything. They got each other looks, which they hadn't been doing for the first 35 minutes. In the end, when it mattered most, they executed brilliantly."

Tyler Brown led the Redbirds with 17 points on 4-of-13 shooting. Hill added 14.

WSU trailed 27-20 at halftime and considered itself fortunate. Illinois State's defense dominate the first 15 minutes of the game, rarely giving the Shockers an open shot or a clear lane to pass. WSU trailed 17-5 after missing 14 of 16 shots and all seven of its three-pointers, mixing in eight turnovers to add to the pain.

BOX SCORE

Wichita State 68 • 22-5 (11-4 MVC)

##	Player		Total FG-FGA	3-Ptr FG-FGA	FT-FTA	Off	Def	Tot	PF	TP	A	TO	Blk	Stl	Min
22	Hall, Carl	f	4-6	0-0	5-6	2	2	4	2	13	0	2	3	1	37
02	Armstead, Malcolm	g	7-16	3-7	1-2	0	6	6	2	18	6	3	0	0	37
05	Williams, Demetric	g	4-11	2-8	0-0	2	5	7	3	10	4	2	1	1	33
21	Orukpe, Ehimen	g	1-2	0-0	1-2	0	2	2	4	3	1	1	1	0	11
32	Cotton, Tekele	g	1-3	0-1	0-0	0	2	2	3	2	2	1	0	1	22
00	Lufile, Chadrack		0-0	0-0	0-2	0	0	0	1	0	0	0	0	0	2
11	Early, Cleanthony		2-6	2-4	6-8	1	2	3	4	12	1	0	0	0	17
15	Wiggins, Nick		1-4	1-3	0-0	1	2	3	1	3	1	0	0	0	15
23	VanVleet, Fred		1-3	1-1	0-0	0	2	2	3	3	0	4	0	1	11
50	White, Jake		2-3	0-0	0-0	2	0	2	2	4	0	1	0	1	15
	Team					1	2	3							
	Totals		23-54	9-24	13-20	9	25	34	25	68	15	14	5	5	200

FG % 1st Half: 8-26   30.8%   2nd half: 15-28 53.6%   Game: 23-54 42.6%
3FG % 1st Half: 2-11 18.2%   2nd half: 7-13 53.8%   Game: 9-24 37.5%
FT % 1st Half: 2-8 25.0%   2nd half: 11-12 91.7%   Game: 13-20 65.0%

Deadball Rebounds 4

Illinois State 67 • 16-11 (8-7 MVC)

##	Player		Total FG-FGA	3-Ptr FG-FGA	FT-FTA	Off	Def	Tot	PF	TP	A	TO	Blk	Stl	Min
13	Wilkins, John	f	1-1	1-1	2-2	0	1	1	3	5	0	0	1	0	21
32	Carmichael, Jackie	f	3-12	0-0	6-7	2	7	9	3	12	0	2	3	1	33
01	Brown, Tyler	g	4-13	0-3	9-10	2	5	7	1	17	3	2	1	1	34
02	Allen, Bryant	g	4-10	1-4	3-3	0	0	0	1	12	2	1	0	0	32
44	Hill, Johnny	g	3-3	0-0	8-9	1	6	7	3	14	2	4	0	2	32
00	Keane, Kaza		0-3	0-1	0-0	1	2	3	1	0	2	1	0	0	17
22	Ekey, Jon		2-4	1-3	2-2	1	2	3	4	7	0	1	1	3	26
24	Upshaw, Zeke		0-2	0-2	0-0	0	0	0	0	0	0	0	0	0	5
	Team					0	2	2				1			
	Totals		17-48	3-14	30-33	7	25	32	16	67	9	12	6	7	200

FG % 1st Half: 6-25 24.0%   2nd half: 11-23 47.8%   Game: 17-48 35.4%
3FG % 1st Half: 2-8 25.0%   2nd half: 1-6 16.7%   Game: 3-14 21.4%
FT % 1st Half: 13-15 86.7%   2nd half: 17-18 94.4%   Game: 30-33 90.9%

Deadball Rebounds 2

Officials: David Hall, Gerry Pollard, Paul Janssen
Technical fouls: Wichita State-None. Illinois State-None.
Attendance: 8668

Score by periods	1st	2nd	Total
Wichita State	20	48	68
Illinois State	27	40	67

	Points	In Paint	Off T/O	2nd Chance	Fast Break	Bench
WSU		26	11	8	0	22
ILS		20	13	2	10	7

Last FG - WSU 2nd-00:06, ILS 2nd-06:15.
Largest lead - WSU by 3 1st-14:33, ILS by 14 1st-07:20.

Score tied - 0 times.
Lead changed - 4 times.

Illinois State's Jackie Carmichael scuffles under the basket with Wichita State's Cleanthony Early and Carl Hall.
By Lori Ann Cook-Neisler, The Pantagraph

WICHITA STATE 66
INDIANA STATE 62

ROAD TO THE TOP
WSU CLOSES IN ON ANOTHER VALLEY CROWN

BY PAUL SUELLENTROP

TERRE HAUTE, Ind. -- Two road wins in three nights tells the rest of the Missouri Valley Conference that Wichita State is serious about winning back-to-back titles. The Shockers didn't win just any road games - they beat the Valley's hottest team on Sunday and backed that up with Tuesday's 66-62 win at Indiana State.

"We control our own destiny, and that's a good position to be in," WSU coach Gregg Marshall said. "I know that it's over, and we've got to win at least one more game."

Tuesday's win maintains a one-game lead over Creighton for WSU (23-5, 12-4 MVC) with two conference games remaining. It can clinch at least a share of the title against Evansville on Feb. 27 at Koch Arena.

If that happens, the Shockers will look back on wins over Illinois State and Indiana State (16-11, 9-7) as the race's turning point. In both, they needed to survive a tough defensive effort by the home team and grit their way to a close victory.

WSU last won back-to-back MVC titles in 1964 and 1965, a fact the players are well aware of. They

Ehimen Orukpe denies Indiana State center Justin Gant in first half action in Terre Haute.
By Jim Avelis, The Tribune-Star

Malcolm Armstead drives to the paint while Indiana State's Jake Odum defends.
By Jim Avelis, The Tribune-Star

Wichita State coach Gregg Marshall reacts to an official's call during the Shockers' 66-62 win at Indiana State.
By Joseph C. Garza, The Tribune-Star

are even more tenacious about defending the program's recent stature atop the conference.

"This program, pretty much, believes that every year we're going to be first," senior Demetric Williams said. "That's our ultimate goal, nothing less."

This one didn't come much easier than Sunday's one-point miracle at Illinois State. WSU needed to make six straight free throws in the final 41 seconds to hold off Indiana State's frantic attempts at its improbable comeback.

Williams made two with 41 seconds to play for a 62-55 lead. After Indiana State's R.J. Mahurin converted a four-point play - fouled by Cleanthony Early on a three - Williams made two more with 33 seconds remaining.

Indiana State's Dawon Cummings sank a long three to cut the lead to 64-62 with 25 seconds to play. The Shockers, after a timeout, passed to Early, who survived a trap in backcourt, drawing a foul call while he tried to elbow his way through.

down, and everybody was telling me to calm down. They see me shoot free throws all the time, so they know."

WSU set the stage with two bursts earlier in the half. Indiana State took a 42-40 lead with a 6-0 run and got the crowd on its feet. The Shockers responded with their own 6-0 run, helped by three turnovers, to go up 46-42 with 8:19 to play.

That sequence kept WSU from falling too far back. It finally knocked the Sycamores back with another 6-0 run, this one to produce a 57-51 lead with 4:04 to play. Carl Hall's three-point play and Malcolm Armstead's three off a Hall's screen gave WSU's its biggest lead.

Early scored 19 points and Armstead added 18. Manny Arop led the Sycamores with 17 points.

"Crazy moment," Early said. "I didn't know what they were going to call."

He made both free throws for a 66-62 lead with 18 seconds to play. Indiana State missed two shots in the final 12 seconds. Early, an 80-percent foul shooter, missed two early in the game and one with 53 seconds to play. Shooting into the student section, most wearing white shirts and holding big heads of celebrities such as Taylor Swift and David Spade, he regrouped.

"I was rushing a couple and they came off my hand a little weird," he said. "I kind of calmed

BOX SCORE

Wichita State 66 • 23-5, 12-4 MVC

##	Player		Total FG-FGA	3-Ptr FG-FGA	FT-FTA	Off	Def	Tot	PF	TP	A	TO	Blk	Stl	Min
22	Hall, Carl	f	4-6	0-0	2-3	1	4	5	1	10	0	0	1	0	34
21	Orukpe, Ehimen	c	0-2	0-0	0-0	0	3	3	2	0	1	0	1	0	16
02	Armstead, Malcolm	g	7-13	4-7	0-0	0	1	1	2	18	3	4	0	3	36
05	Williams, Demetric	g	2-6	0-1	8-9	1	6	7	4	12	2	1	0	0	33
32	Cotton, Tekele	g	0-2	0-1	0-0	0	2	2	4	0	1	1	1	1	14
00	Lufile, Chadrack		0-0	0-0	0-0	0	0	0	0	0	0	0	1	0	1
11	Early, Cleanthony		6-14	4-8	3-6	1	3	4	3	19	0	0	0	1	32
15	Wiggins, Nick		1-4	0-3	5-6	1	1	2	2	7	1	0	0	1	22
23	VanVleet, Fred		0-4	0-1	0-0	1	1	2	0	0	2	1	0	2	10
50	White, Jake		0-1	0-0	0-0	0	1	1	0	0	0	1	0	0	2
	Team					1	3	4				1			
	Totals		20-52	8-21	18-24	6	25	31	18	66	10	9	4	8	200

FG % 1st Half: 8-25 32.0% 2nd half: 12-27 44.4% Game: 20-52 38.5%
3FG % 1st Half: 4-12 33.3% 2nd half: 4-9 44.4% Game: 8-21 38.1%
FT % 1st Half: 5-6 83.3% 2nd half: 13-18 72.2% Game: 18-24 75.0%

Deadball Rebounds 3

Indiana State 62 • 16-11, 9-7 MVC

##	Player		Total FG-FGA	3-Ptr FG-FGA	FT-FTA	Off	Def	Tot	PF	TP	A	TO	Blk	Stl	Min
05	Gant, Justin	f	2-4	1-2	2-4	0	0	0	0	7	1	0	0	0	26
31	Mahurin, R.J.	c	4-8	2-6	3-3	1	2	3	2	13	1	1	0	1	28
03	Arop, Manny	g	4-11	2-5	7-8	2	7	9	2	17	1	1	1	2	35
12	Cummings, Dawon	g	3-9	1-4	1-2	0	6	6	1	8	1	7	0	1	25
13	Odum, Jake	g	6-11	1-1	2-6	0	6	6	4	15	5	3	0	1	36
00	Kitchell, Jake		0-0	0-0	0-0	0	3	3	0	0	0	1	0	0	10
02	Eitel, Lucas		0-2	0-1	0-0	1	2	3	1	0	0	0	0	1	13
11	Brown, Devonte		0-1	0-0	0-0	0	1	1	1	0	1	1	0	0	13
32	Smith, Khristian		1-3	0-0	0-0	4	0	4	5	2	1	1	0	0	14
	Team					0	2	2				1			
	Totals		20-49	7-19	15-23	8	29	37	16	62	11	16	1	6	200

FG % 1st Half: 9-24 37.5% 2nd half: 11-25 44.0% Game: 20-49 40.8%
3FG % 1st Half: 3-10 30.0% 2nd half: 4-9 44.4% Game: 7-19 36.8%
FT % 1st Half: 4-6 66.7% 2nd half: 11-17 64.7% Game: 15-23 65.2%

Deadball Rebounds 4

Officials: Scott Thornley, Mark Whitehead, Hal Lusk
Technical fouls: Wichita State-None. Indiana State-None.
Attendance: 6169

Score by periods	1st	2nd	Total
Wichita State	25	41	66
Indiana State	25	37	62

	Points In Paint	Off T/O	2nd Chance	Fast Break	Bench
WSU	20	13	9	0	26
INS	22	14	3	4	2

Last FG - WSU 2nd-02:11, INS 2nd-00:25.
Largest lead - WSU by 8 2nd-02:11, INS by 3 1st-18:45.

Score tied - 11 times.
Lead changed - 9 times.

CREIGHTON 91
WICHITA STATE 79

McDARNIT

CREIGHTON STAR KILLS WSU'S MVC TITLE HOPES

BY PAUL SUELLENTROP

O MAHA -- Wichita State couldn't score against Evansville. It couldn't play defense against Creighton.

That is the recipe for a disappointing end to the regular season for the Shockers, who blew a one-game lead with two to play and ended up as a prop for Creighton's senior-day celebration in Saturday's 91-79 loss at the CenturyLink Center. Creighton won the Missouri Valley Conference title, in front of 18,613 fans, and the loss stuck WSU in second place.

Not bad for a team picked fourth in the preseason, but not good with the way it ended.

The Shockers (24-7, 12-6 MVC) will go to the conference tournament in St. Louis knowing they kicked away a precious conference title by losing 59-56 at home to Evansville on Wednesday. Then the Bluejays (24-7, 13-5) ran over them with a scoring explosion for the ages.

Junior forward Doug McDermott scored 41 points on 15-of-18 shooting and Creighton made 33 of 47 shots (70.2 percent), the best by an opponent in WSU history.

WSU's Demetric Williams goes up for two and the foul against Creighton's Grant Gibbs.
By Fernando Salazar, Wichita Eagle

Creighton's Doug McDermott muscles WSU's Tekele Cotton in the second half at the Century Link Center.
By Fernando Salazar, Wichita Eagle

"This team is built on defense and rebounding," WSU guard Demetric Williams said. "We let their best player get off. It's all on how he starts, and we let him start off good. It's hard to stop a good player once he gets going."

Oscar Robertson scored 50 against the Shockers in 1958 and Larry Bird went for 49 in 1979. Add McDermott's name to that list.

WSU tried everything and none of it slowed him down. He made three-pointers. He scored in the lane, getting great position and working over and through defenders. He made one outrageous three after a step-back dribble and all the Shockers could do was watch and try to get a hand in his face.

"He was special," WSU coach Gregg Marshall said. "I mean, 41 points on 18 shots, that's spectacular."

Everything about the Bluejays looked that way, and against a tough defensive team. The Shockers played well on offense and couldn't keep up.

Creighton made 20 of 28 shots in the second half and scored 55 points. The 91 points are the most given up in regulation by a Marshall-coached team at WSU.

"With what was on the line against a big rival, it just doesn't get much better than this," McDermott said. "The coaching staff deserves a lot of credit for putting together a good scouting report."

Creighton's starters made 27 of 37 shots. Guard Austin Chatman scored 12 points, as did forward

WSU's Demetric Williams tries to steal the ball from Creighton's Austin Chatman in the second half at the Century Link Center in Omaha. *By Fernando Salazar, Wichita Eagle*

Grant Gibbs. Forward Ethan Wragge came off the bench to make 3 of 4 threes, two back-breakers in the second half.

"Offensively, they were so good," Marshall said. "They were spectacular. We tried just about every-

thing in our arsenal."

WSU's Williams tied a career-high with 18 points. The Shockers scored 49 second-half points, making 16 of 25 shots. Even at that clip, they couldn't trade baskets.

WSU's Cleanthony Early can barely watch as the Shockers fall to Creighton 91-79 and fall to second place in the MVC standings.
By Fernando Salazar, Wichita Eagle

"They didn't miss shots," WSU guard Malcolm Armstead said. "There's not much you can do when you can't gets stops."

Creighton's offense hit a high gear in the second half and WSU couldn't keep up. Even when Mc-Dermott went to the bench, the Bluejays kept rolling. A 13-5 run gave them a 66-54 lead and forced Marshall to call timeout with 8:23 remaining.

After that, Creighton's Grant Gibbs threw in a desperation shot, while falling out of bounds, at the shot-clock buzzer for a 69-54 lead.

At that point, Marshall said he looked at Creighton coach Greg McDermott in wonderment, who returned a shrug.

WSU rallied, cutting the lead to 71-65. That only sparked another Bluejay burst, with Doug Mc-Dermott getting open for threes. He made one over Carl Hall for a 74-65 lead. One from the corner, uncontested, gave Creighton a 77-66 lead.

WSU started the first half looking timid and unsure how to attack. It missed four three-pointers in the first five minutes. After a timeout, a shot-clock violation made the Shockers look even more off track. Creighton built an 11-4 lead, with McDermott scoring nine of those points.

It took a burst of defense for WSU to look serious about winning. Armstead's three-pointer cut Creighton's lead to 19-15. His steal led to a dunk by Cleanthony Early. Then the Shockers played a ferocious 30 seconds of defense, with Williams wrestling with McDermott in the lane, before Creighton's Avery Dingman missed a contested three. Tekele Cotton's three gave the Shockers their first lead at 20-19.

WSU took its biggest lead of the half, 27-23, on a follow shot by Hall. Early picked up his second foul with 4:23 remaining and exited, handing momentum back to Creighton. It finished the half on a 12-4 run to lead 36-31.

BOX SCORE

Wichita State 79 • 24-7, 12-6 MVC

##	Player		Total FG-FGA	3-Ptr FG-FGA	FT-FTA	Off	Def	Tot	PF	TP	A	TO	Blk	Stl	Min
22	Hall, Carl	f	5-8	0-0	5-6	4	2	6	2	15	3	1	1	1	31
21	Orukpe, Ehimen	c	0-1	0-0	0-0	0	2	2	3	0	0	1	1	1	16
02	Armstead, Malcolm	g	2-8	2-5	0-0	0	1	1	1	6	5	1	0	1	30
05	Williams, Demetric	g	6-14	1-7	5-5	1	3	4	1	18	6	2	0	1	34
32	Cotton, Tekele	g	5-7	4-5	0-2	0	3	3	4	14	2	1	0	4	31
11	Early, Cleanthony		4-8	0-4	3-4	1	1	2	3	11	0	2	0	1	21
15	Wiggins, Nick		1-1	0-0	0-0	0	1	1	0	2	0	1	0	0	9
23	VanVleet, Fred		2-2	0-0	0-0	1	0	1	1	4	3	0	0	1	15
50	White, Jake		4-6	0-0	1-1	0	0	0	1	9	0	0	0	1	13
	Team					0	1	1				1			
	Totals		29-55	7-21	14-18	7	14	21	16	79	19	10	2	11	200

FG % 1st Half: 13-30 43.3% 2nd half: 16-25 64.0% Game: 29-55 52.7%   Deadball
3FG % 1st Half: 2-10 20.0% 2nd half: 5-11 45.5% Game: 7-21 33.3%   Rebounds
FT % 1st Half: 3-3 100.0 2nd half: 11-15 73.3% Game: 14-18 77.8%   1

Creighton 91 • 24-7, 13-5 MVC

##	Player		Total FG-FGA	3-Ptr FG-FGA	FT-FTA	Off	Def	Tot	PF	TP	A	TO	Blk	Stl	Min
03	McDermott, Doug	f	15-18	5-8	6-6	1	5	6	2	41	3	3	0	0	32
00	Echenique, Gregory	c	4-4	0-0	1-2	0	4	4	3	9	0	0	0	0	26
01	Chatman, Austin	g	4-8	1-2	3-3	0	2	2	2	12	6	2	0	0	35
10	Gibbs, Grant	g	4-5	1-2	3-3	0	3	3	2	12	8	4	0	0	32
12	Manigat, Jahenns	g	0-2	0-2	0-0	0	3	3	2	0	0	1	0	1	36
02	Stormberg, Taylor		0-0	0-0	0-0	0	0	0	0	0	0	0	0	0	0+
11	Yates, Andre		0-0	0-0	0-0	0	1	1	0	0	1	1	0	0	3
22	Dingman, Avery		1-4	1-3	0-0	0	2	2	2	3	0	1	0	0	14
30	Kelling, Joe		0-0	0-0	0-0	0	0	0	0	0	0	1	0	0	0+
31	Artino, Will		2-2	0-0	1-2	1	1	2	1	5	2	0	0	0	10
34	Wragge, Ethan		3-4	3-4	0-0	0	1	1	1	9	1	0	0	1	12
40	Olsen, Alex		0-0	0-0	0-0	0	0	0	0	0	0	0	0	0	0+
	Team					0	0	0							
	Totals		33-47	11-21	14-16	2	22	24	15	91	21	13	0	2	200

FG % 1st Half: 13-19 68.4% 2nd half: 20-28 71.4% Game: 33-47 70.2%   Deadball
3FG % 1st Half: 3-7 42.9% 2nd half: 8-14 57.1% Game: 11-21 52.4%   Rebounds
FT % 1st Half: 7-9 77.8% 2nd half: 7-7 100.0 Game: 14-16 87.5%   0

Officials: Hal Lusk, Terry Davis, Randy Heimerman
Technical fouls: Wichita State-None. Creighton-None.
Attendance: 18613
Senior Day for Creighton's Echenique, Stormberg, Jones, Gibbs & Kelling.
Second-largest home crowd in Creighton MBB history.
Creighton clinches first outright MVC title since 2000-01.

Score by periods	1st	2nd	Total
Wichita State	31	48	**79**
Creighton	36	55	**91**

	Points	In Paint	Off T/O	2nd Chance	Fast Break	Bench
WSU		30	19	6	14	26
CU		42	17	4	2	17

Last FG - WSU 2nd-00:12, CU 2nd-00:28.
Largest lead - WSU by 4 1st-04:38, CU by 16 2nd-01:02.

Score tied - 3 times.
Lead changed - 4 times.

SHOCKERS FEATURE
CLEANTHONY EARLY

EARLY'S RISE AT WSU COMES FAR AWAY FROM HOME

BY BOB LUTZ

Sandra Glover will forever mourn, as does a mother who loses a son.

It's been 2½ years since the eldest of her two boys, Jamel Glover, drowned in Schoharie Creek, near Charleston, N.Y. He had been swimming with friends and slipped as he tried to get out of the water, according to reports. As others helped, Glover, 32, panicked and pulled them under as well. He had a wife, two kids and a third on the way.

"Oh, wow, I have my moments," Sandra Glover said. "I have my days."

And when she does, Glover remembers the wise words spoken to her by her youngest son, Cleanthony Early, Wichita State's junior scoring machine who scored 39 points, the most by a Shocker in 27 years, last week against Southern Illinois.

"He told me, 'Mom, God does things for a reason,'" Glover said. "He said we don't know why, but things happen for a reason. I asked him what the reason could be and Cleanthony said, 'Mom, we don't know and we may never know.' He said God doesn't make mistakes."

Jamel Glover was more than a big brother to Early, he was a father figure. He first put a basketball in Early's hands and encouraged Early to dribble it.

"Cleanthony is quiet, he internalizes," Sandra Glover said. "He holds it in for a long time, but at Jamel's service he broke down. He couldn't take it so

WSU's Cleanthony Early shows off his shirt as they celebrate after defeating Gonzaga 76-70 during the third round of the NCAA Tournament in Salt Lake City.
By Fernando Salazar, Wichita Eagle

he had to leave."

But Early didn't check out. He had just finished a year at Mount Zion Academy in North Carolina, unable to attend a Division I school out of Pine Bush (N.Y.) High because of poor grades.

That year at Mount Zion changed him, his mother said. He had never been a troublemaker, but he also lacked direction.

"He came back from Mount Zion a different person," Sandra Glover said. "He grew up in the church with me and his grandmother."

It wasn't until that year at Mount Zion, though, that spirituality spilled into Early's being. The school's religious instruction got his attention and it's because of that, he believes, that he was able to be a rock for his mother in the confusion of such tragedy.

"My parents were separated when I was young, so I followed my brother around all the time," Early said. "But after he was gone, it was like I became the protector of the family."

Instead of going far off to college to play college basketball, Early decided to stay close to home and played two seasons at Sullivan Community College in Middletown, N.Y. There are three junior college divisions and Sullivan is Division III, low on the pecking order. College recruiters don't make a path to places like Sullivan.

But Early made the best of a difficult situation. He wanted to be close to his mom during such a traumatic time while also giving basketball the attention it deserved so that he could eventually earn a Division I scholarship. Mission accomplished in both areas: Early was a two-time Division III player of the year at Sullivan and finally narrowed his dozens of college choices to San Diego State, Baylor, Alabama, Washington State and Wichita State.

Wherever he was going, he would be far away from home. He thought he was ready.

His mother wasn't.

"I didn't want to let Cleanthony out of my sight," Glover said. "I was doing so much praying, asking the Lord not to let my baby get too far away."

Early, though, knew Wichita State was the place for him. He was recruited heavily by Shocker assistant Greg Heier, who sold Anthony on what the Shockers were and what they were becoming.

Early arrived with a reputation as a scorer. He averaged 20 points as a senior at Pine Bush, 24 at Mount Zion, 20.4 as a freshman at Sullivan and 24.2 as a sophomore.

"How good can he be?" Wichita State coach Gregg Marshall contemplated. "I don't know that I can determine his ceiling. He can certainly continue to improve and he's pretty good right now."

Early has reached double figures in 13 of the Shockers' 16 games. But his 39-point explosion against Southern Illinois took his a relatively calm season and transformed it into Hurricane Cle.

"I woke up the next morning to quite a few more text messages and quite a few more notifications on Facebook and Twitter," Early said. "There are the ones you know who have always been with you and I'm thankful for the new supporters."

Early, who loves to read – another passion he picked up during his time at Mount Zion – isn't a normal college Twitter enthusiast. His tweets are often philosophical and represent his deep religious faith. He's as much fun as the next guy, those who know him say, but he has a serious undertone, molded from his life experiences.

Basketball has been an outlet for Early. He's naturally gifted and now willing to put in the hard work that will help him discover how good he can be.

"I believe I can go all the way, whatever level I'm on," Early said. "I'm going to always work and do what I need to do to get to where I need to be. I thank God every single day that I'm not where I was, but also not where I want to be."

Marshall said he coached a couple of players with NBA ability at Winthrop, and that three of the Shocker seniors last season – Garrett Stutz, Joe Ragland and Toure Murry – were close.

Early, though, looks like he could be on a different level.

"He can score in a lot of ways," Marshall said. "I told him after the Bradley game (24 points) that what I love about you is how good you are right now, but also how much better you can be. It's exciting for me and it's exciting for him. He was like a wild colt when he came to us. You don't want to break that spirit, but you want to get him running in the right direction."

WICHITA STATE 69
MISSOURI STATE 59

BACK TO BASICS
REBOUNDING, DEFENSE LEAD WSU TO VICTORY

BY PAUL SUELLENTROP

S T. LOUIS -- Quarterfinal victories are routine for Wichita State in the Missouri Valley Conference Tournament. Now for the real obstacle, the one that regularly seems to frustrate the Shockers and their fans in the Scottrade Center.

Second-seeded Wichita State defeated seventh-seeded Missouri State 69-59 on Friday. The Shockers (25-7) face Illinois State in the semifinals, a traditional pit of despair for highly seeded WSU teams. It is 1-6 in semifinal games since 2003. Four times, it failed to advance past Saturday as a No. 1 or No. 2 seed.

WSU's first priority on Friday was to end a two-game losing streak in which its defense faltered. With its identity restored, the Shockers can take on the rest of the tournament with a newly fortified bench and continued rebounding dominance.

"We're getting back to the roots, back to defensive intensity," forward Jake White said. "Everyone is starting to communicate again and we're really playing well."

Missouri State (11-21) stayed in the game at the

WSU's Cleanthony Early drives to the basket for two against Missouri State in the second half in St. Louis.
By Fernando Salazar, Wichita Eagle

Ron Baker returned for Wichita State after missing much of the season with a stress fracture.
By Fernando Salazar, Wichita Eagle

foul line, making 23 free throws. The Shockers shut down their half-court offense by keeping the Bears out of the lane and forcing them to shoot a lot of guarded three-pointers. They missed 14 of 18 and shot 37.2 percent from the field. While they pushed WSU until the final minutes, the Bears couldn't get closer than six points in the final six minutes.

The Shockers out-rebounded the Bears 43-24, grabbing 20 offensive rebounds and scoring 22 second-chance points. Carl Hall led WSU with 18 points and 12 rebounds. Ron Baker, returning from a stress fracture that sidelined him since Dec. 13,

scored 15 points in 19 minutes.

"We simply couldn't keep them off the glass," MSU coach Paul Lusk said. "Their best offense sometimes is a missed shot and it certainly was true today."

Valley Freshman of the Year Marcus Marshall led MSU with 25 points. He made 13 of 16 free throws and 4 of 10 threes.

Baker energized WSU's offense with his shooting - 3 of 5 from behind the arc - and his passing. The Shockers left most everything else to Hall and Jake White, who pushed the smaller Bears around in the lane. White scored nine points and grabbed eight rebounds, four on the offensive end. Several times they teamed up to rebound the other's miss and keep possessions alive until one of them scored.

"(Hall) goes to the glass every single time, so normally he brings two or three people with him just to try and box him out," White said. "That leaves the weak side open a lot and I just capitalized on that."

The Bears, despite tired legs from Thursday's game, stayed close and Marshall's three tied the game 46-all with 7:56 remaining. Hall's offensive rebound led to a jumper for White to start an 8-0 run. Fred VanVleet added a three and Baker's layup, on an assist from White, made it 54-46 with 5:45 to play.

Big plays from reserves - White, VanVleet and Baker - helped WSU all night. Its bench produced 36 points, even with leading scorer Cleanthony Early returning to the starting lineup.

"We were deeper, because we added Ron Baker back to the fold," WSU coach Gregg Marshall said. "We had tremendous production from guys who played 10 to 15 minutes a game. Tonight, they played a little more."

The Shockers fell behind early in the first half, a victim of poor shooting. Their defense and rebounding took over late in the half and the Shockers led 29-24 at the break.

WSU close the half on an 8-1 run. Nick Wiggins tied the game 23-all on a jumper by Wiggins. Baker scored on an assist from Malcolm Armstead and Wiggins' runner gave the Shockers a 27-23 lead. After a Bears foul shot, Hall's putback made it 29-24.

WSU missed all eight of its three-pointers in the first half, but their size advantage paid off with a 12-rebound edge and 10 second-chance points on nine offensive rebounds. Hall scored seven points, grabbing four offensive boards.

The bench gave the Shockers a big lift. Marshall went to his reserves early in the half. They scored 17 points, and that was without Early's usual contribution, since he started.

WSU's Cleanthony Early defends against Missouri State's Keith Pickens in the first half during the Missouri Valley Tournament.
By Fernando Salazar, Wichita Eagle

BOX SCORE

Missouri State 59 - 11-22; 7-11 MVC

##	Player		Total FG-FGA	3-Ptr FG-FGA	FT-FTA	Off	Def	Tot	PF	TP	A	TO	Blk	St	Min
00	DOWNING,ANTHONY	g	3-11	0-2	6-6	1	3	4	4	12	1	1	0	0	33
01	PICKENS,KEITH	f	4-7	0-0	3-5	1	4	5	1	11	2	1	1	2	40
11	MARSHALL,MARCUS	g	4-11	4-10	13-16	0	3	3	3	25	2	2	0	0	39
30	SCHEER,NATHAN	g	0-5	0-5	1-2	0	1	1	5	1	0	3	0	0	29
42	KIRK,CHRISTIAN	f	2-4	0-0	0-0	2	3	5	4	4	0	0	0	0	36
03	SIMPSON,MICHAEL		0-0	0-0	0-0	0	0	0	0	0	0	0	0	0	1
10	AROMONA,TOMIE		0-0	0-0	0-0	0	0	0	0	0	0	0	0	0	1
15	WILSON,DREW		0-0	0-0	0-0	0	0	0	2	0	0	0	0	0	2
20	THURMAN,GAVIN		3-5	0-1	0-0	0	3	3	1	6	0	2	0	1	19
	TEAM					2	1	3		0					
	Totals		16-43	4-18	23-29	6	18	24	20	59	5	9	1	3	200

FG % 1st Half: 7-23 30.4% 2nd Half: 9-20 45.0% Game: 16-43 37.2% Deadball
3FG % 1st Half: 1-8 12.5% 2nd Half: 3-10 30.0% Game: 4-18 22.2% Rebounds
FT % 1st Half: 9-13 69.2% 2nd Half: 14-16 87.5% Game: 23-29 79.3% 4,0

Wichita State 69 - 25-7; 12-6 MVC

##	Player		Total FG-FGA	3-Ptr FG-FGA	FT-FTA	Off	Def	Tot	PF	TP	A	TO	Blk	St	Min
02	ARMSTEAD,MALCOLM	g	1-7	0-3	2-2	0	2	2	2	4	5	1	0	0	31
05	WILLIAMS,DEMETRIC		1-3	0-2	0-0	0	3	3	3	2	0	1	0	0	20
11	EARLY,CLEANTHONY	f	2-8	0-1	1-1	3	1	4	3	5	2	1	0	0	21
22	HALL,CARL	f	6-11	0-0	6-11	9	3	12	2	18	0	1	1	0	31
32	COTTON,TEKELE	g	2-5	0-2	0-2	0	1	1	4	4	0	0	1	1	13
15	WIGGINS,NICK		3-5	0-1	0-0	1	0	1	1	6	1	1	0	1	21
21	ORUKPE,EHIMEN		1-2	0-0	1-2	1	5	6	2	3	0	3	1	0	7
23	VANVLEET,FRED		1-1	1-1	0-0	0	0	0	2	3	3	0	0	0	17
31	BAKER,RON		5-7	3-5	2-2	0	2	2	2	15	2	1	0	0	19
50	WHITE,JAKE		4-8	0-1	1-1	4	4	8	1	9	3	2	0	0	20
	TEAM					2	2	4		0					
	Totals		26-57	4-16	13-21	20	23	43	21	69	16	11	2	2	200

FG % 1st Half: 12-27 44.4% 2nd Half: 14-30 46.7% Game: 26-57 45.6% Deadball
3FG % 1st Half: 0-8 00.0% 2nd Half: 4-8 50.0% Game: 4-16 25.0% Rebounds
FT % 1st Half: 5-7 71.4% 2nd Half: 8-14 57.1% Game: 13-21 61.9% 1,0

Officials: Scott Thornley, Gerry Pollard and Tom O'Neill
Technical Fouls: Missouri State- None. Wichita State- None.
Attendance: 0

Score by periods	1st	2nd	Total
Missouri State	24	35	59
Wichita State	29	40	69

Points	In Paint	Off T/O	2nd Chance	Fast Break	Bench
Missouri State	18	10	4	2	6
Wichita State	36	15	4	0	36

Largest lead - Missouri State by 6 1st-15:50; Wichita State by 11 2nd-05:18

Score tied - 6 times
Lead changed - 3 times

WICHITA STATE 66
ILLINOIS STATE 51

THE ARCH RIVAL AWAITS
SHOCKERS LOCK DOWN ILLINOIS STATE, FACE CREIGHTON FOR MVC TITLE

BY PAUL SUELLENTROP

S T. LOUIS -- Wichita State's defense won the moment Illinois State's Tyler Brown launched a guarded and long three-pointer for no reason other than frustration. The bad shot missed badly and the Shockers turned that bad decision into a beautifully executed fast break and a three-point play.

Game over. No more comebacks for the Redbirds, who couldn't run their offense and couldn't score for long stretches against WSU. The Shockers defended and rebounded their way to a 66-51 victory in the semifinals of the Missouri Valley Conference Tournament, landing them in the championship game against top-seeded Creighton on Sunday.

Second-seeded Wichita State (26-7) is one win away from locking up an NCAA Tournament berth. It is one win away from leaving St. Louis - after 22 years of irrelevancy, heartbreak and frustration - happy.

All because the Shockers dialed up one of their best defensive efforts of the season, one on par with a win at Virginia Commonwealth and a smothering of Iowa in Mexico. At times this season, WSU got

WSU's Demetric Williams goes up for two against Illinois State's Johnny Hill in the first half at the Scottrade Center. *By Fernando Salazar, Wichita Eagle*

WSU's Malcolm Armstead, left, steals the ball from Illinois State's Johnny Hill in the first half during their semifinal game of the MVC Tournament in St. Louis. *By Fernando Salazar, Wichita Eagle*

away from that all-out effort. In this tournament, that style is back.

"You could tell from the beginning of the game our defense was going to go," guard Demetric Williams said. "When we get out on them and guard them from the beginning, you can tell we're ready."

The Shockers held sixth-seeded Illinois State (18-15) to its lowest points total this season and its worst shooting percentage (29.1) this season. They out-rebounded the Redbirds 48-31.

Carl Hall led WSU with 16 points and eight rebounds. Malcolm Armstead added 15 points and three steals.

Armstead started with two steals in the first two minutes, forcing Redbirds coach Dan Muller to take out point guard Johnny Hill. Hall blocked shots and single-covered Jackie Carmichael much of the game, helping his teammates stick with shooters. Tekele Cotton wore on Brown, denying him the ball and keeping a hand in his face with a defen-

sive masterpiece. Cleanthony Early, playing sick, blocked three shots.

Armstead's sticky hands and WSU's press threw off the Redbirds, who didn't see that much pressure in the regular season. The Shockers built a 17-1 lead, forcing misses and luring the Redbirds into rushed shots.

"They came out ready to roll," Muller said. "We turned the ball over. They jumped on us."

The Redbirds didn't score a field goal until Brown's layup, after a steal, with 7:25 remaining in the first half, cutting WSU's lead to 22-8. They didn't score against WSU's half-court defense until Jon Ekey's three with 5:13 remaining. The Redbirds, helped by a switch to a zone defense, rallied and took the lead before trailing 26-24 at halftime. In the second half, WSU figured out the zone by getting the ball inside and passing more crisply. Their defense continued to frustrate the Redbirds.

The Shockers shut down one of the Valley's top scoring teams. Carmichael, an All-MVC pick, scored 22 points, but missed six free throws and fouled out late in the game. Brown, after scoring 28 points in Friday's quarterfinal, scored nine and went 3 for 12 from three-point range.

"Cotton did a great job," Muller said. "Tyler's been face-guarded for the last four or five games and we found a way to get him the ball. We were having a hard time getting him the ball on plays we usually run for him."

Cotton, a sophomore guard, made sure of that. He rarely helped off Brown, who averages 18.4 points, and denied him the ball all over the court.

"It was our coaching staff's plan to X him out, so that's what we did," Cotton said.

With Cotton on his mind, Brown took an ill-fated shot midway through the second half with the Redbirds trailing 45-36. The Shockers rebounded and broke. Ron Baker shoveled a pass to Carl Hall, who laid the ball in over Carmichael. Referee Don Daily over-ruled a charging foul because Carmi-

chael set up in the restricted circle under the basket. Carmichael went to the bench with his fourth foul and Hall's free throw gave the Shockers a 48-36 lead with 11:25 remaining.

With the Redbirds broken, WSU extended the lead to as many as 17.

"This (Illinois State) is a prolific scoring team when they've got it going," WSU coach Gregg Marshall said. "We were not only getting stops, we were so active in cleaning the glass and getting in transition. This was a defensive effort that can get you to a championship game and, hopefully, help you win it."

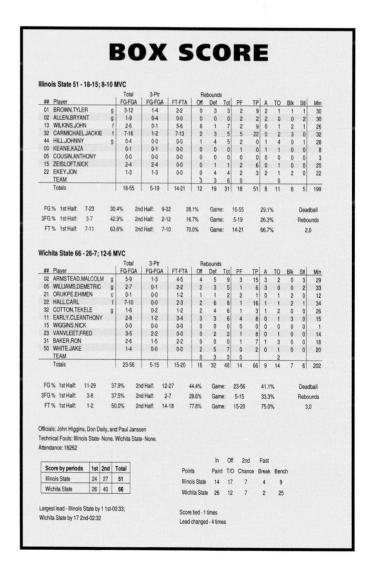

WSU's Tekele Cotton goes up for two against Illinois State during the MVC Tournament semifinal.
By Fernando Salazar, Wichita Eagle

CREIGHTON 68
WICHITA STATE 65

WSU FALLS IN FINAL
SHOCKERS MISS ON CHANCE TO TIE GAME IN FINAL SECONDS

BY PAUL SUELLENTROP

ST. LOUIS -- Wichita State held Creighton under 70 points, out-rebounded the Bluejays and watched Doug McDermott miss more than half his shots.

Close, but still not enough to beat the top-seeded Bluejays in the Missouri Valley Conference Tournament, an event that could be re-named the Creighton Invitational if the school's future didn't appear to be in another conference.

Creighton defeated second-seeded WSU 68-65 in Sunday's championship game at the Scot-trade Center. WSU lost for the second time in the title game in 23 trips to St. Louis. Creighton won its 12th tournament title and the Valley's auto-matic bid to the NCAA Tournament.

"It's hard when you have all the emotions that go into a game like that," WSU coach Gregg Marshall said. "The initial disappointment is paramount. We tip our hat to Creighton for mak-ing one more play. It came down to a three-point shot to tie the game."

Wichita State's Cleanthony Early shoots over Creighton's Gregory Echenique during the second half.
By Travis Heying, Wichita Eagle

Wichita State's Carl Hall tries to get to the basket against Creighton's Doug McDermott during the second half.
By Travis Heying, Wichita Eagle

WSU (26-8) is expected to receive one of 37 at-large bids to the NCAA Tournament next Sunday. If selection committee members watched - CBS cut away from the final minutes in most of the country for the Indiana-Michigan game - they saw a resilient team that pushed Creighton (27-7) to the final second.

If reports are correct, Creighton will soon exit the Valley for the Big East. If so, the rivals sent out the series with tons of drama and physical play.

"It's just an unbelievable rivalry we have with Wichita State," Creighton coach Greg McDermott said. "I don't think there's a lot of love lost between us, but I think there's a lot of respect between us."

Malcolm Armstead's off-balance three for WSU hit the rim and bounced away in the final second to end the game and bring a rush of Creighton fans onto the court. Armstead turned and grimaced at the painful end to a wonderful game. He scored a career-high 28 points and kept WSU's offense afloat through difficult times.

Down three with 12 seconds to play, Marshall elected not to call time-out and let Armstead run a play selected during a time-out nine seconds earlier. WSU ran the same pick-and-pop play that worked for a game-winning three by Cleanthony Early at Illinois State. Creighton defended it well, not allowing Armstead to pass and making him shoot a guarded shot over the 6-foot-8 McDermott.

"I took a tough shot and didn't convert it,"

Armstead said. "I came off the screen and they switched it and that's why I didn't get a good look like I should have."

McDermott was ready for the play.

"We knew Armstead was probably going to get that shot," he said. "We were switching ball screens with him all game. I stuck with that, switched on to him and tried to get a hand in his face without fouling him. Luckily, he missed."

The Shockers trailed most of the game, even while holding Creighton's offense in check compared to a 91-79 loss in the regular-season finale. The Bluejays led 66-55 when WSU made it interesting. Armstead and Ron Baker made two threes. Carl Hall made a foul shot to cut the lead to 66-62. Another three by Armstead brought the Shockers within 66-65 with 43 seconds remaining.

"You just have to keep playing," Early said. "You can't look at the scoreboard and lose hope."

Creighton's Jahenns Manigat made a layup, barely slipping it by Hall's block attempt, for a 68-65 lead with 21 seconds to play.

"I kind of got a fingertip on it," Hall said. "I was guarding McDermott and he just made it hard for me because you can't help. You've got to stay with him."

The Shockers did that for much of the game. McDermott burned them for 41 points in Omaha. Sunday, he scored 14 on 5-of-13 shooting and missed all three of his three-pointers. Creighton made 41.5 percent of its shots, way below its usual rate, but made 11 of 24 threes. Manigat led the Bluejays with a season-high 16 points. Ethan Wragge came off the bench to make five threes and score 15 points. Manigat got loose early in the second half with two threes to build an eight-point lead for Creighton.

One burst from McDermott was enough for Creighton. He scored five straight points to give the Bluejays a 37-30 lead and grab momentum early in the second half. Bluejay shooters did the rest. Manigat made two threes to stretch the lead to 44-35. Wragge's three over Ehimen Orukpe put Creighton up 47-39. Grant Gibbs made one for a 52-43 lead.

Creighton's Gregory Echenique shoots for two against WSU's Carl Hall in the second half during the championship game of the MVC Tournament at the Scottrade Center in St. Louis. *By Fernando Salazar, Wichita Eagle*

BOX SCORE

Wichita State 65 • 26-8; 12-6 MVC

##	Player		Total FG-FGA	3-Ptr FG-FGA	FT-FTA	Off	Def	Tot	PF	TP	A	TO	Blk	Stl	Min
22	Hall, Carl	f	4-14	0-0	5-8	5	1	6	2	13	1	0	4	0	32
21	Orukpe, Ehimen	c	0-2	0-0	0-0	2	1	3	0	0	0	1	1	0	13
02	Armstead, Malcolm	g	10-20	4-9	4-5	2	7	9	1	28	3	1	0	4	35
05	Williams, Demetric	g	0-5	0-4	0-0	0	3	3	3	0	1	2	0	1	28
32	Cotton, Tekele	g	3-4	1-2	1-2	2	4	6	1	8	0	0	1	0	24
11	Early, Cleanthony		1-5	0-1	0-1	2	2	4	4	2	0	1	0	0	23
15	Wiggins, Nick		2-3	1-2	0-0	0	0	0	0	5	0	0	0	1	5
23	VanVleet, Fred		0-1	0-0	0-0	0	0	0	0	0	0	0	0	0	9
31	Baker, Ron		3-7	1-3	0-0	4	2	6	4	7	1	0	0	0	19
50	White, Jake		0-6	0-0	2-2	1	1	2	1	2	1	0	0	0	12
	Team					2	1	3							
	Totals		23-67	7-21	12-18	20	22	42	16	65	7	5	6	6	200

FG % 1st Half: 11-34 32.4% 2nd half: 12-33 36.4% Game: 23-67 34.3%
3FG % 1st Half: 2-11 18.2% 2nd half: 5-10 50.0% Game: 7-21 33.3%
FT % 1st Half: 4-7 57.1% 2nd half: 8-11 72.7% Game: 12-18 66.7%

Deadball Rebounds 1

Creighton 68 • 27-7; 13-5 MVC

##	Player		Total FG-FGA	3-Ptr FG-FGA	FT-FTA	Off	Def	Tot	PF	TP	A	TO	Blk	Stl	Min
03	McDermott, Doug	f	5-13	0-3	4-5	0	4	4	3	14	0	2	0	0	28
00	Echenique, Gregory	c	3-7	0-0	3-4	7	4	11	4	9	1	2	6	0	32
01	Chatman, Austin	g	0-5	0-2	1-2	0	2	2	1	1	7	1	0	2	36
10	Gibbs, Grant	g	3-6	2-2	3-5	1	5	6	3	11	7	1	0	0	36
12	Manigat, Jahenns	g	6-11	4-8	0-0	0	5	5	2	16	3	2	1	0	39
22	Dingman, Avery		0-1	0-0	0-0	0	2	2	0	0	0	1	0	0	9
31	Artino, Will		0-1	0-0	2-4	3	2	5	2	2	0	0	0	0	4
34	Wragge, Ethan		5-9	5-9	0-0	0	1	1	1	15	0	0	0	0	16
	Team					1	4	5							
	Totals		22-53	11-24	13-20	12	29	41	16	68	18	9	7	2	200

FG % 1st Half: 10-29 34.5% 2nd half: 12-24 50.0% Game: 22-53 41.5%
3FG % 1st Half: 6-14 42.9% 2nd half: 5-10 50.0% Game: 11-24 45.8%
FT % 1st Half: 4-6 66.7% 2nd half: 9-14 64.3% Game: 13-20 65.0%

Deadball Rebounds 4

Officials: Scott Thornley, Mike Stuart, and Don Daily
Technical fouls: Wichita State-None. Creighton-None.
Attendance: 16659
MVC Tournament championship game.
Doug McDermott named MVP; Gregory Echenique named All-Tournament Team too.

Score by periods	1st	2nd	Total
Wichita State	28	37	65
Creighton	30	38	68

	Points	In Paint	Off T/O	2nd Chance	Fast Break	Bench
WSU		26	9	19	4	16
CU		20	4	8	0	17

Last FG - WSU 2nd-00:43, CU 2nd-00:12.
Largest lead - WSU by 1 1st-02:15, CU by 13 2nd-05:12.

Score tied - 1 time.
Lead changed - 2 times.

SHOCKERS FEATURE

COACH GREGG MARSHALL

MARSHALL READY FOR MOMENT

BY BOB LUTZ

S ALT LAKE CITY -- Gregg Marshall has a chance Saturday night to add a 10-carat diamond to a gold-studded career as a basketball coach that started in 1985.

The 50-year-old Marshall spent Friday making the media rounds as a guest on ESPN Radio's "Mike and Mike" show, followed by an appearance on "The Jim Rome Show."

He and Wichita State are one of the flavors of the minute in college basketball, a stick of Juicy Fruit just after it's been put into your mouth.

But we all know how fleeting that sweet taste can be. So, after thumping Pittsburgh by 18 points in the NCAA Tournament's second round Thursday, Marshall and his Shockers now step to the center stage, under the brightest lights, to play the No. 1 team in the country. Gonzaga.

They crave another taste of limelight.

This is where 28 years in coaching has led Marshall. To this game, this night, with a chance to make an even bigger name for himself and create a buzz Wichita State basketball hasn't experienced in a long time.

"It's a moment, yeah, a big game," Marshall said.

But that's about all he said about the potential

WSU coach Gregg Marshall has a few words with Cleanthony Early during the opening victory over Pittsburgh in the NCAA Tournament.
By Fernando Salazar, Wichita Eagle

Wichita State coach Gregg Marshall yells at the crowd after cutting down the net at the end of the West Regional Final at Staples Center in Los Angeles. *By Travis Heying, Wichita Eagle*

ramifications of the game because he's caught up in preparation, not hyperventilation.

Marshall is aware of the game's significance. Friday, he went national. Beat Gonzaga and he and the Shockers go international, the talk of the basketball universe.

Which, I'm guessing, is a notion met with some resistance by WSU basketball fans. Of course they want a Shocker win over the Zags. What they could do without is the certain chatter of Marshall and his coaching future that would

undoubtedly follow.

It's the catchiest of Catch-22s, a game that has been played frequently at WSU throughout the Marshall and Mark Turgeon years.

Shocker fans should be assured that Marshall and his family - wife, Lynn and two kids, sophomore Kellen and seventh-grader Maggie - love being in Wichita. They loved being in Rock Hill, S.C., for nine seasons while Marshall coached at Winthrop.

"He's happy where he's at," said WSU associate head coach Chris Jans. "He's not a guy who thinks the grass is always greener. It's not coach-speak when he talks about his affinity for Wichita State and how much he likes and wants to be here. He loves it here."

The Shockers will be going up against a Gonzaga team coached by Mark Few, in his 14th season as the team's coach. For 10 years before that, he was an assistant.

Few often exclaims his love for Spokane and Gonzaga, to the point now where nobody even considers him leaving. Of course, 15 consecutive NCAA Tournaments have proven he can win at Gonzaga as much as he can win almost anywhere else.

Marshall is finishing his sixth season at WSU. The Shockers have won 108 games in the past four.

"You can't buy happy and we're happy," Marshall said. "We're very comfortable here. I have two kids who view Wichita as their home. They didn't want to leave South Carolina and now they don't want to leave Wichita. And that's a factor for me.

"I make these things a family choice. I don't just say, 'Hey, pack your bags, here we go. Daddy's been offered $2 million to go get his brains beaten out over here for three years before he gets fired.' That's not what I want to do. I like winning and I think we're going to win here."

The Marshall you see pacing the sidelines, shaking his wrist to re-position his watch, reaching for a security blanket in the form of a cup of a Gatorade-water mix, is an indication of the man's tirelessness.

"He's always on," Jans said of his boss. "There's never a day when he's in the office or at practice that he's not trying to improve the program in any way he can find. It could be a big thing, it could be a small thing. But he's always looking for some way to give our team an advantage."

Marshall pushes buttons. He pushes envelopes. And he pushes everybody who plays or works for him.

It's not unusual to see him scream at a player or even one of his assistants during a game, in public for everyone to see. Imagine what practices must be like.

What are they like?

Freshman Fred VanVleet needed a moment to come up with a word.

"It's like ... torture... ," he said. "But it's fun, it's fun."

Sounds like a real blast.

"As long as you keep things in perspective, then you'll get through it," VanVleet continued. "But if you're just thinking about practice that day, it's going to kill you. He puts us through some tough times, but obviously it's paying off now. There's a method to all that madness."

There's a basketball promised land, and the Shockers are climbing steps to get there. First a 25-win season in 2009-10, then an NIT championship in 2011-12. Last season, WSU made it to the NCAA Tournament, losing in the first round to VCU.

Now they have a tourney win and a chance at the model non-BCS basketball program in the country. Gonzaga.

The Shockers haven't played a No. 1 team in 45 seasons. They haven't beaten one in more than 50.

"It's a wonderful opportunity," Marshall said.

He didn't want to go much deeper than that. He doesn't want the game to be more about his legacy than his team's chance to keep the season alive.

But there's no downplaying the significance of Wichita State-Gonzaga.

"You'd have to ask him about the importance of a game like this," Jans said. "But in my opinion, I think we all realize the magnitude and what it could do for Coach Marshall. And more importantly, what it does for Wichita State's program."

This one is in prime time. Everybody who loves college basketball and the NCAA Tournament will be watching. The Shockers are on the cusp of doing something special with a coach who knows how to seize the moment.

You won't want to miss this one.

WSU coach Gregg Marshall instructs his team during their game with Evansville at Koch Arena.
By Fernando Salazar, Wichita Eagle

WICHITA STATE 73
PITTSBURGH 55

BULLYING THE BIG GUYS
WSU KNOCKS OUT BIGGER PITT WITH POWER, SPEED

BY PAUL SUELLENTROP

SALT LAKE CITY -- Wichita State matched Pittsburgh's power and over-matched it with quickness, an asset nobody outside the coaching staff saw coming.

The ninth-seeded Shockers handled Pittsburgh 73-55, routing the Big East's fourth-place team with surprising ease in the second round of the NCAA Tournament's West Regional at EnergySolutions Arena. That win, a mild upset by seeding, will get the Shockers some attention for a lockdown defensive performance.

One more will bring all the basketball-following nation around to WSU. It plays top-seeded Gonzaga on Saturday with the winner advancing to the regional semifinals, better known as the Sweet 16.

WSU coach Gregg Marshall told the Shockers they made him proud. He told them their toughness won the day. Then he challenged them to extend their stay in the tournament with a trip to Los Angeles.

"Are you satisfied?" he said. "Are we done? Are we going to celebrate now like this is the end? Or are you going to continue to push through, and let's try to head to where ever the next round is."

The Shockers (27-8) played like a team that

Wichita State forward Carl Hall grabs a rebound in the second half against Pittsburgh.
By Jaime Green, Wichita Eagle

WSU's Tekele Cotton steals the ball from Pitt's Trey Ziegler, left, and Tray Woodall in the second half during the second round of the NCAA Tournament in Salt Lake City. *By Fernando Salazar, Wichita Eagle*

won't be satisfied easily. They bullied the eighth-seeded Panthers and led by 11 or more points the final 6:49. WSU's effort - and his team's lack of effort - mystified Pitt coach Jamie Dixon.

"They were far more aggressive than us," he said. "I can't explain it."

An attempt: The Shockers smacked the disinterested Panthers early in the game and refused to

let them regroup. By the time the Panthers discovered their urgency, WSU grabbed control and closed out with a parade of dunks and free throws. Pitt missed 16 of 17 three-pointers and shot 35.2 percent for the game.

Guard Malcolm Armstead led WSU with 22 points, 11 in the final seven minutes. Forward Cleanthony Early shook off a disappointing con-

ference tournament to add 21. The Shockers made 11 of 21 shots in the second half, enough to survive shooting 2 of 20 from three-point range.

"Going into the game, Coach made the statement 'Knock 'em in the face first,' " Early said. "That's what we tried to do."

WSU out-rebounded the Big East's top rebounding team 37-32. It grabbed 11 offensive rebounds to produce 14 second-chance points and help outscore Pitt 33-16 at the foul line.

If the power game kept it even, speed allowed WSU to run away. It scored 21 points off 15 turnovers against a normally careful team.

"One of our strengths is low turnovers, and for people who haven't seen us play, this wasn't our team," Dixon said. "We had five or six turnovers early that were not typical of how we play and put us in a hole."

WSU coaches watched video of Pitt and came away impressed with its size. They also believed the Shockers could bother the Panthers with their quickness. Guard Tekele Cotton jumped passing lanes and harassed dribblers to record five steals. He rounded out that performance by blanketing guard Tray Woodall, who scored two points on 1-of-12 shooting before fouling out 10 points under his team-leading average.

Cotton provided the first of two killer bursts with steals on consecutive possessions midway through the second half. He stole a pass from Trey Zeigler, caught unaware while trying to start a play near the three-point line, and dunked for a 45-35 lead, provoking a leg kick in celebration from Marshall. Another steal led to free throws for Early and a 12-point edge with 10:13 remaining.

"Those are huge baskets," Marshall said. "In a game like that, low points, if you can steal baskets.... You don't want to give those freebies."

Assistant coach Chris Jans had told Marshall that WSU's quickness could disrupt the Panthers.

Again and again, it did that by taking advantage of sloppy passes and weak handles. Pitt surrendered double-digit steals for the third time this season.

"Pressure," Armstead said. "Tekele did real good setting the tempo. We just built off that and got some easy baskets."

Armstead finished off the Panthers late. He banked in a shot for a 50-39 lead. After two missed foul shots by Pitt, he slithered into the lane for a lefty layup off the glass, drawing a foul. His three-point play put WSU up 53-49 with 5:43 remaining.

When the Panthers pressed, he sliced through it and found Early for a dunk and a 55-40 lead. The Panthers never got closer than 13 points.

WSU's Cleanthony Early fights for a rebound against Pittsburgh in the first half during the NCAA Tournament in Salt Lake City. *By Fernando Salazar, Wichita Eagle*

BOX SCORE

Wichita State 73 • 27-8

##	Player		Total FG-FGA	3-Ptr FG-FGA	FT-FTA	Off	Def	Tot	PF	TP	A	TO	Blk	Stl	Min
22	Hall, Carl	f	3-6	0-0	5-6	2	4	6	3	11	0	2	0	0	24
21	Orukpe, Ehimen	c	0-1	0-0	1-2	2	2	4	3	1	0	2	0	0	15
02	Armstead, Malcolm	g	6-14	1-6	9-9	2	1	3	2	22	5	1	0	1	28
31	Baker, Ron	g	0-5	0-5	6-8	0	2	2	4	6	3	2	0	1	29
32	Cotton, Tekele	g	2-3	1-2	1-2	0	3	3	0	6	2	0	0	5	33
00	Lufile, Chadrack		1-1	0-0	0-0	0	0	0	1	2	0	1	0	1	6
05	Williams, Demetric		0-2	0-1	3-4	0	1	1	2	3	0	1	0	1	14
11	Early, Cleanthony		7-15	0-6	7-8	3	4	7	2	21	0	1	1	1	28
15	Wiggins, Nick		0-0	0-0	0-0	0	1	1	0	0	0	0	0	0	3
23	VanVleet, Fred		0-2	0-0	1-2	1	2	3	1	1	1	0	0	0	14
50	White, Jake		0-0	0-0	0-0	0	0	0	1	0	0	1	0	0	6
	Team					1	6	7							
	Totals		19-49	2-20	33-41	11	26	37	20	73	11	11	1	10	200

FG % 1st Half: 8-28 28.6% 2nd half: 11-21 52.4% Game: 19-49 38.8%
3FG % 1st Half: 1-14 7.1% 2nd half: 1-6 16.7% Game: 2-20 10.0%
FT % 1st Half: 9-12 75.0% 2nd half: 24-29 82.8% Game: 33-41 80.5%

Deadball Rebounds 6

Pittsburgh 55 • 24-9

##	Player		Total FG-FGA	3-Ptr FG-FGA	FT-FTA	Off	Def	Tot	PF	TP	A	TO	Blk	Stl	Min
21	Patterson, Lamar	f	1-7	0-4	7-7	0	0	0	5	9	2	3	0	1	21
42	Zanna, Talib	f	1-4	0-0	2-4	4	3	7	2	4	0	1	0	0	20
13	Adams, Steven	c	5-7	0-0	3-4	3	8	11	2	13	1	1	2	1	27
00	Robinson, James	g	2-7	0-3	3-3	0	1	1	4	7	3	2	0	0	30
01	Woodall, Tray	g	1-12	0-5	0-0	1	4	5	5	2	1	5	0	0	30
03	Wright, Cameron		3-4	0-0	0-0	1	0	1	2	6	0	0	0	1	14
05	Johnson, Durand		1-5	1-3	0-0	0	1	1	4	3	0	0	1	0	19
11	Taylor, Dante		2-3	0-0	1-2	0	0	0	1	5	0	1	0	0	13
23	Zeigler, Trey		0-0	0-0	0-0	0	2	2	1	0	0	2	1	0	6
44	Moore, J.J.		3-5	0-2	0-0	0	0	0	1	6	0	0	0	1	20
	Team					2	2	4							
	Totals		19-54	1-17	16-20	11	21	32	27	55	8	15	5	5	200

FG % 1st Half: 7-23 30.4% 2nd half: 12-31 38.7% Game: 19-54 35.2%
3FG % 1st Half: 0-7 0.0% 2nd half: 1-10 10.0% Game: 1-17 5.9%
FT % 1st Half: 7-8 87.5% 2nd half: 9-12 75.0% Game: 16-20 80.0%

Deadball Rebounds 2

Officials: Verne Harris, Brian Dorsey, Rod Dixon
Technical fouls: Wichita State-None. Pittsburgh-None.
Attendance:

Score by periods	1st	2nd	Total
Wichita State	26	47	**73**
Pittsburgh	21	34	**55**

WICHITA STATE 76
GONZAGA 70

SHOCKIN' AWE
WSU RALLIES TO KNOCK OFF NO. 1 GONZAGA, GET IN SWEET 16

BY PAUL SUELLENTROP

SALT LAKE CITY -- Wichita State knocked off No. 1 and is headed to Los Angeles as one of the biggest stories of the NCAA Tournament.

Two outrageously nervy three-pointers by two big-stage ready freshmen stunned top-ranked and top-seeded Gonzaga, lifting Wichita State to a 76-70 win at EnergySolutions Arena in the third round of the NCAA Tournament's West Regional.

Ninth-seeded WSU (28-8) knocked off a No. 1 team for the first time since 1963 with a blend of three-point shooting and gritty defense. After the win, they celebrated in a mosh pit at halfcourt, surrounded by cameras. Gonzaga (32-3) walked silently off the court, paralyzed by a meltdown in the final minutes.

"This feeling is unimaginable," WSU freshman Ron Baker said.

Senior Carl Hall could only smile.

"I can't even hardly talk right now," he said. "I can't describe this feeling. It's crazy."

Words were not needed when the buzzer sounded. The black-and-yellow celebration on the court said it

WSU's Carl Hall dunks the ball against Gonzaga in the first half of the NCAA Tournament.
By Fernando Salazar, Wichita Eagle

WSU's Carl Hall battles for a rebound with Gonzaga's Kelly Olynyk in the second half during the third round of the NCAA Tournament. *By Fernando Salazar, Wichita Eagle*

all. Cleanthony Early chest-bumped Chadrack Lu-file. Baker stood alone near halfcourt, arms raised in celebration.

The Shockers posed for pictures, hugged fans and danced to the "Shocker War Chant" in front of the pep band. Coaches danced. Athletic director Eric Sexton danced. Family members danced. The band chanted "We going to L.A."

Everybody danced. It was a night for dancing, Shocker style, in the Big Dance.

Next up for WSU is a trip to the Staples Center to face either 12th-seeded Mississippi or 13th-seeded La Salle on Thursday.

"Just a euphoric feeling," WSU coach Gregg Marshall said. "It was just awesome. It was a natural reaction for me, really, hugging the people that I care about and letting them know."

WSU wrote one of the biggest wins in its basketball history by rallying from a 49-41 deficit with under 12 minutes remaining. It appeared Gonzaga

WSU's Cleanthony Early starts a fast break for the Shockers in the first half during the third round of the NCAA Tournament in Salt Lake City. *By Fernando Salazar, Wichita Eagle*

had the momentum and the pedigree to shrug off the spunky challengers. It did not, largely because of a hail of three-pointers.

Baker started the rally with a three after a time-out to cut the lead to 49-44. Early added one to bring WSU within 51-48. The Shockers kept coming from long range, using threes by Tekele Cotton, Early (16 points) and Baker (16 points) to get within 61-60 and force a timeout with 4:14 to play.

After a Kelly Olynyk miss, contested heavily by Hall, Hall made a 15-foot jumper to give the Shockers a 62-61 lead. A foul on Baker gave him two free throws for a 64-63 lead with 3:10 to play.

Then Gonzaga unraveled, starting with a mental error of the highest order.

After the free throws, guard Kevin Pangos tossed the ball inbound to David Stockton, who walked out of bound to pass the ball in. The referees caught it — with Marshall yelling for the violation — and gave the ball to WSU. Baker's corner three made it 67-63. After two Gonzaga free throws, freshman Fred VanVleet (13 points) made a long three over Stockton with the shot clock winding down for a 70-65 lead.

"A definite miscommunication," Gonzaga coach Mark Few said. "A really bad time for that to happen."

Gonzaga responded with another turnover, a wild pass up court that Olynyk tried to save. VanVleet made two free throws with 38.6 seconds to play for a 72-65 lead. Stockton's layup cut WSU's lead to 72-67.

Malcolm Armstead made two free throws with 15.2 seconds remaining for a 74-67 lead and the Shockers started celebrating. VanVleet added two more with 11.2 seconds remaining.

WSU, after going 2 of 20 from three-point range in Thursday's win over Pittsburgh, made 14 of 28. Baker made 4 of 6. Early made 4 of 7. Cotton and VanVleet each added two.

The Shockers held Gonzaga to 35.6-percent shooting. Olynyk scored 26 points, needing 22 shots to get there. Pangos made 6 of 17 shots and scored 19 points.

The second half started ominously for WSU. Early picked up his third foul going for a rebound less than a minute into the half. Carl Hall got his third with 17:50 remaining. Gonzaga started the half on

a 6-2 run to cut WSU's lead to 38-37 with 15:09 to play. Fouls continued to mount, much to the displeasure of WSU fans and coaches. Jake White screamed after being called for a charge that handed the ball to Gonzaga.

WSU momentarily regained its footing with a press. Four Shockers surrounded Pangos and clawed the ball away. VanVleet's three-point play stopped Gonzaga's run and gave WSU a 41-37 lead.

It didn't last long.

Pangos made WSU pay for a switch to a zone defense, burying a three from the wing. After an airball by Early, Mike Hart sank a corner three for a 43-41 lead and forced a timeout. A WSU turnover led to a jumper by Olynyk and the burst continued. Pangos stole the ball from Hall, trying to spin in the lane, and scored for a 49-41 lead.

BOX SCORE

Wichita State 76 • 28-8

##	Player		Total FG-FGA	3-Ptr FG-FGA	FT-FTA	Off	Def	Tot	PF	TP	A	TO	Blk	Stl	Min
22	Hall, Carl	f	3-6	0-0	2-6	1	0	1	3	8	2	3	3	1	29
21	Orukpe, Ehimen	c	1-2	0-0	0-1	1	0	1	2	2	0	2	1	0	15
02	Armstead, Malcolm	g	2-9	1-6	3-4	0	5	5	1	8	3	3	0	2	37
31	Baker, Ron	g	5-7	4-6	2-2	3	3	6	2	16	4	1	0	1	33
32	Cotton, Tekele	g	3 5	2-3	0-0	1	2	3	2	8	2	0	0	2	25
00	Lufile, Chadrack		0-0	0-0	0-0	0	0	0	1	0	0	1	0	0	1
05	Williams, Demetric		0-1	0-1	0-0	0	0	0	2	0	1	0	0	0	7
11	Early, Cleanthony		6-11	4-7	0-0	2	5	7	4	16	1	2	2	1	24
23	VanVleet, Fred		3-6	2-4	5-5	0	1	1	1	13	3	1	0	1	20
50	White, Jake		2-3	1-1	0-0	1	2	3	4	5	0	2	0	0	9
	Team					1	2	3							
	Totals		25-50	14-28	12-18	10	20	30	22	76	16	15	6	8	200

FG % 1st Half: 14-29 48.3% 2nd half: 11-21 52.4% Game: 25-50 50.0%
3FG % 1st Half: 7-15 46.7% 2nd half: 7-13 53.8% Game: 14-28 50.0%
FT % 1st Half: 1-2 50.0% 2nd half: 11-16 68.8% Game: 12-18 66.7%
Deadball Rebounds 3

Gonzaga 70 • 32-3

##	Player		Total FG-FGA	3-Ptr FG-FGA	FT-FTA	Off	Def	Tot	PF	TP	A	TO	Blk	Stl	Min
13	Olynyk, Kelly	f	8-22	0-3	10-14	6	3	9	1	26	2	4	1	1	38
20	Harris, Elias	f	2-8	1-2	7-8	4	3	7	2	12	1	3	0	3	35
04	Pangos, Kevin	g	6-17	4-12	3-5	0	0	0	4	19	5	4	0	3	39
05	Bell Jr., Gary	g	0-2	0-1	0-0	0	2	2	0	0	0	1	0	0	21
30	Hart, Mike	g	2-3	2-2	0-0	7	7	14	4	6	1	0	0	0	27
03	Dranginis, Kyle		0-0	0-0	0-0	0	1	1	1	0	1	0	0	0	8
11	Stockton, David		2-2	0-0	0-0	2	0	2	0	4	3	0	0	0	17
35	Dower, Sam		0-2	0-1	0-0	0	0	0	3	0	0	1	1	0	6
43	Barham, Drew		1-3	1-2	0-2	1	0	1	2	3	0	0	0	1	9
	Team					1	2	3							
	Totals		21-59	8-23	20-29	21	18	39	17	70	13	13	2	8	200

FG % 1st Half: 9-28 32.1% 2nd half: 12-31 38.7% Game: 21-59 35.6%
3FG % 1st Half: 3-12 25.0% 2nd half: 5-11 45.5% Game: 8-23 34.8%
FT % 1st Half: 10-13 76.9% 2nd half: 10-16 62.5% Game: 20-29 69.0%
Deadball Rebounds 6

Officials: John Higgins, Brian Dorsey, John Gaffney
Technical fouls: Wichita State-None. Gonzaga-None.
Attendance: 16060

Score by periods	1st	2nd	Total
Wichita State	36	40	76
Gonzaga	31	39	70

BEYOND SWEET
FIRST NCAA REGIONAL FINAL IN 32 YEARS AWAITS AFTER SHOCKERS PUT EARLY BEATING ON LA SALLE

BY PAUL SUELLENTROP

LOS ANGELES -- Wichita State got giddy after advancing to the Sweet 16. Moving on to the Elite Eight produced a more measured response, one from a team that is suddenly experienced winning big games and knows it needs at least one more.

WSU advanced to the regional finals of the NCAA Tournament - the Elite Eight - for the first time since 1981 with Thursday's 72-58 win over La Salle at Staples Center in a West Regional semifinal.

No dancing. No curtain calls with the band. The Shockers hugged, clapped and smiled. They looked like a team that wants to cut down nets on Saturday and really let loose.

"We need one more win to seal this deal," WSU guard Ron Baker said.

The ninth-seeded Shockers (29-8) will play second-seeded Ohio State on Saturday in the West Regional final, with the winner headed to

Wichita State guard Malcolm Armstead takes a shot against La Salle during the first half of the West Regional semifinal at Staples Center.
By Travis Heying, Wichita Eagle

Wichita State guard Ron Baker grabs a rebound over La Salle's Rohan Brown.
By Travis Heying, Wichita Eagle

Atlanta for the Final Four. WSU is 40 minutes away from the national semifinals, a height reached in 1965. The 1964 and 1981 Shockers lost in regional finals, falling one game short of the Final Four.

WSU is the first Missouri Valley Conference team to make the Elite Eight since the 1981 team, which defeated Kansas in the Sweet 16 before losing to LSU in New Orleans. Indiana State, in 1979, is the last MVC Final Four team.

All that, and perhaps more, is two halves away for WSU.

"Forty minutes away," WSU guard Malcolm Armstead said. "It's a dream come true."

Armstead led WSU with 18 points, 13 in the second half. Carl Hall added 16, 14 in the first half. WSU out-rebounded La Salle 47-29, helping it to a 40-26 edge scoring in the lane.

The Shockers decided this one early, establishing their dominance in the lane with height and aggressiveness. The team that made "Play Angry" its motto and answered the "Are you satisfied" question from its coach in the negative came out hungry. They led 14-2 and the Explorers (24-10) never recovered. Hall scored 10 of those points.

"That was the game plan," Armstead said. "We tried to wear them down, pound it inside."

La Salle looked worn down throughout the game, both because of WSU's hustle and, perhaps, because of its travel schedule. The Explorers had to win three games last week.

"I think we were a little fresher and I think we were beating them down the floor," WSU coach Gregg Marshall said.

WSU guard Ron Baker, right, dives for a loose ball against La Salle's Ramon Galloway.
By Travis Heying, Wichita Eagle

"Carl Hall set the tone with just out-running their bigs."

La Salle's four-guard offense failed to generate consistent scoring with WSU's guards bottling them up. When they slipped through, Hall and others blocked and altered shots. The Shockers held the Explorers (24-10) to 35.7-percent shooting.

"WSU won the game in the first half," La Salle coach John Giannini said. "They really overwhelmed us. It took us a half to adjust to the level they were playing at."

Ramon Galloway, La Salle's leading scorer, failed to shed WSU's Tekele Cotton and had 11 points on 4-of-15 shooting. Forward Jerrell Wright and guard Tyrone Garland both scored 16.

The Shockers won with Hall in the first half, overpowering the smaller Explorers on their way to 38-22 lead. They hit them with three-pointers early in the second half. When the Explorers briefly rallied midway through the second half, Armstead took over with nine straight points to take the life out of La Salle. His three-pointer gave WSU a 62-47 lead with 6:40 to play.

"Armstead was huge at that time," Giannini said. "We were playing well enough at that time to have a chance, but Armstead wouldn't allow it."

A follow shot by Ron Baker and a layup by Cotton made it 66-48. Seconds later, Giannini called timeout and fans started leaving. Another Explorers turnover led to a layup by Early and the WSU fans started celebrating with a 20-point lead.

WSU was on its way to the Elite Eight with a blowout. The celebration unfolded in subdued fashion compared to Saturday's scene in Salt Lake City after beating Gonzaga. Marshall cuffed assistant coach Chris Jans around the

Wichita State's Carl Hall fights for a rebound against La Salle's Tyrone Garland.
By Travis Heying, Wichita Eagle

Malcolm Armstead and Carl Hall walk off the court after beating La Salle 72-58 to advance to the West Regional final.
By Travis Heying, Wichita Eagle

head with a big smile. The players clapped and hugged. They looked more focused on the next game than popping jerseys and dancing with the band.

The Shockers played just as sharply to begin the second half.

WSU forced a La Salle timeout just over a minute into the second half with three-pointers by Armstead and Baker. Those baskets stretched WSU's lead to 44-22, its largest of the game, and inspired the band into playing the "Shocker War Chant."

La Salle refused to roll over, sparked by unexpected baskets in the lane by Jerrell Wright. He spent most of the first half on the bench with two fouls. In the second half, La Salle got him the ball and he converted two free throws, a three-point play and a layup to cut WSU's lead to 44-29. Then Galloway sank a long three-pointer to complete a 10-0 run.

Baker's three, on a break, stopped the run gave WSU a 47-22 lead. The Explorers kept coming, however, helped when Hall picked up his third foul after setting a screen and running over a defender with 13 minutes remaining. La Salle cut the lead to 49-38 on a three-point play by Tyreek Duren.

WSU made its size advantage work from the tip, going small without really going small. Early replaced center Ehimen Orukpe in the lineup. The Shockers rode Hall, who scored 10 of their first 14 points on the way to a 14-2 lead. Hall scored twice on lobs over the defender, once on a follow shot and once off a bounce pass from Armstead on a break.

Fred VanVleet's three-pointer, with the shot clock running down, gave WSU a 17-3 lead. The Shockers made 8 of their first 12 shots, holding the Explorers to 2-of-11 shooting at the 11:49 mark to lead 17-6.

The Explorers made one run in the first half, cutting WSU's lead from 25-12 to 25-17. The Shockers quickly regained control and then pulled away again. Early's drive and basket started an 11-2 run to end the half and give WSU a 38-22 lead.

WSU's final eight minutes of near-perfect execution against Gonzaga flowed almost seamlessly into the first half. It made 16 of 30 shots and out-rebounded the Explorers 26-12. WSU dominated with its size, outscoring La Salle 24-10 in the lane.

Hall scored 14 points in the first half, making 7 of 8 shots, and grabbing six rebounds.

WSU held Galloway to five points on a 2-of-9 shooting in the first half. Tekele Cotton spent most of the half shadowing Galloway, forcing him into two airballs. Armstead, Baker and Demetric Williams also took turns guarding him. Tyrone Garland led La Salle with eight points, making 2 of 10 shots.

BOX SCORE

La Salle 58 - 24-10

##	Player		Total FG-FGA	3-Ptr FG-FGA	FT-FTA	Off	Def	Tot	PF	TP	A	TO	Blk	Stl	Min
01	PETERSON,DJ	g	0-0	0-0	0-0	0	0	0	1	0	0	1	0	0	20
03	DUREN,TYREEK	g	3-7	0-1	2-3	1	1	2	2	8	4	1	1	0	37
10	MILLS,SAM	g	2-8	1-4	2-2	2	1	3	2	7	0	0	0	0	33
25	WRIGHT,JERRELL	f	6-9	0-0	4-5	1	4	5	3	16	0	3	0	0	22
55	GALLOWAY,RAMON	g	4-15	2-6	1-2	0	8	8	2	11	3	4	0	2	38
05	DUNN,TAYLOR		0-0	0-0	0-0	0	0	0	0	0	0	0	0	0	1
13	HUNT,GARVIN		0-0	0-0	0-0	0	0	0	0	0	0	0	0	0	1
21	GARLAND,TYRONE		5-15	4-7	2-4	0	4	4	1	16	1	0	0	2	31
35	BROWN,ROHAN		0-2	0-0	0-0	1	0	1	2	0	0	1	1	1	17
	TEAM					4	2	6	0			0			
	Totals		20-56	7-18	11-16	9	20	29	13	58	8	9	2	5	200

FG % 1st Half: 8-30 26.7% 2nd Half: 12-26 46.2% Game: 20-56 35.7% Deadball
3FG % 1st Half: 3-8 37.5% 2nd Half: 4-10 40.0% Game: 7-18 38.9% Rebounds
FT % 1st Half: 3-6 50.0% 2nd Half: 8-10 80.0% Game: 11-16 68.8% 2,1

Wichita State 72 - 29-8

##	Player		Total FG-FGA	3-Ptr FG-FGA	FT-FTA	Off	Def	Tot	PF	TP	A	TO	Blk	Stl	Min
02	ARMSTEAD,MALCOLM	g	7-15	2-3	2-2	0	6	6	2	18	4	2	1	2	29
11	EARLY,CLEANTHONY	f	4-11	0-1	0-0	3	4	7	1	8	1	1	0	0	27
22	HALL,CARL		7-11	0-0	2-3	3	5	8	3	16	1	3	0	0	27
31	BAKER,RON	g	4-6	2-3	3-4	2	2	4	1	13	2	1	1	1	34
32	COTTON,TEKELE	g	3-7	0-2	0-0	1	3	4	2	6	2	0	1	0	28
00	LUFILE,CHADRACK		0-1	0-0	0-0	0	2	2	0	0	0	0	0	0	6
05	WILLIAMS,DEMETRIC		0-2	0-1	0-0	1	2	3	2	0	0	0	0	0	15
15	WIGGINS,NICK		1-2	0-0	0-0	1	0	1	0	2	0	0	0	0	5
21	ORUKPE,EHIMEN		1-3	0-0	0-0	4	5	9	1	2	0	1	1	0	8
23	VANVLEET,FRED		3-9	1-2	0-0	0	0	0	1	7	2	0	0	1	18
50	WHITE,JAKE		0-0	0-0	0-0	0	0	0	0	0	0	0	0	0	3
	TEAM					2	1	3	0			0			
	Totals		30-67	5-12	7-9	17	30	47	13	72	12	8	8	4	200

FG % 1st Half: 16-30 53.3% 2nd Half: 14-37 37.8% Game: 30-67 44.8% Deadball
3FG % 1st Half: 1-5 20.0% 2nd Half: 4-7 57.1% Game: 5-12 41.7% Rebounds
FT % 1st Half: 5-7 71.4% 2nd Half: 2-2 100.0% Game: 7-9 77.8% 1,0

Officials: Terry Wymer, Lamont Simpson, Ron Groover
Technical Fouls: La Salle- None. Wichita State- None.
Attendance: 18232
2013 NCAA Men's D1 Basketball West Regional Semifinal

Score by periods	1st	2nd	Total
La Salle	22	36	58
Wichita State	38	34	72

Points	In Paint	Off T/O	2nd Chance	Fast Break	Bench
La Salle	26	6	7	0	16
Wichita State	40	11	7	9	11

Largest lead - La Salle by ;
Wichita State by 22 2nd-18:48

Score tied - 1 times
Lead changed - 0 times

WICHITA STATE 70
OHIO STATE 66

FOURTITUDE

SHOCKERS FIGHT OFF OHIO STATE TO EARN SPOT IN THE FINAL FOUR

BY PAUL SUELLENTROP

LOS ANGELES — Wichita State coach Gregg Marshall stood on the ladder and counted down to the crowd of fans in Staples Center.

"Four," he yelled, holding up four fingers. "Two. One."

"Four. Two. One."

"Four. Two. One."

Wichita State can play angry all the way to Atlanta for the Final Four after Saturday's 70-66 win over second-seeded Ohio State. The Shockers believe they can play angry all the way to the NCAA title.

The ninth-seeded Shockers (30-8) finished their march through the regional with a tour de force of aggression, determination and spirit properly channeled. They cut down nets, posed for pictures with the West Regional trophy and quickly talked about finishing in the Georgia Dome, where they expect to cut down more nets.

"Happiness throughout my whole body," WSU freshman Ron Baker said. "It's my (20th) birthday and we're going to the Final Four."

Wichita State players hold up the West Regional Final trophy at Staples Center in Los Angeles. The Shockers earned a berth in the Final Four for the first time since 1965.
By Travis Heying, Wichita Eagle

Above: Senior Carl Hall and freshman Fred VanVleet celebrate after beating Ohio State in the West Regional final in Los Angeles. *By Jaime Green, Wichita Eagle*

Following Page: Wichita State Shockers guard Fred VanVleet scrambles for a loose ball against Ohio State's Aaron Craft. *By Travis Heying, Wichita Eagle*

The Shockers are in the Final Four. Next up is two and then one.

"It feels good, but we're not done yet," senior Carl Hall said. "It's on to the next game. We're just ready to go and make a run for this thing."

WSU knocked off the top two seeds in the region on its way to its first Final Four since 1965. It will play the winner of Sunday's Duke-Louisville game on Saturday.

Coach Gregg Marshall hugged Lynn, his wife, before cutting down the nets. It took him 15 seconds to control his emotions before summing it up.

"Awesome," he said. "It's great. So many people were positive that first year (2007-08). I remember getting a standing ovation ... after we lost a game at home. Because we were playing our butts off. We've got some of the most loyal fans. They deserve this more than you know."

The Shockers won a school-record 30th game with 35 minutes of superb play and five holding on for dear life to earn the biggest road trip of their careers.

Ohio State (29-8) made a late push, pressing and tiring out the Shockers. It got within three points before WSU pushed back. Tekele Cotton's three gave WSU a 65-59 lead. Then his offensive rebound — beating bigger players to the ball — gave the Shockers possession. That ended with Fred VanVleet's shot in the lane bouncing on the rim once, twice, three times before settling in for a 67-61 lead. After an Aaron Craft miss, Ron Baker made two free throws for a 69-61 lead with 51.3 seconds to play.

"We needed a bucket," VanVleet said. "Probably not the most pretty shot, but it went for me."

Malcolm Armstead led WSU with 14 points. Early and VanVleet each added 12.

Ohio State forward Deshaun Thomas goes up against the defense of Wichita State's Tekele Cotton and Carl Hall.
By Travis Heying, Wichita Eagle

Baker scored nine points, all from the foul line.

La Quinton Ross led Ohio State with 19 points. Ohio State shot 31.1 percent for the game. It fell behind in the first half with a miserable shooting performance, 8 of 33 and 2 of 10 from three-point range.

"Man, they D'd us up," Buckeyes coach Thad Matta said. "You can't go 8 for 31 in the first half of a great team."

WSU made strong starts a trademark this tournament. It took the fight to Pittsburgh in its opener. It led top-seeded Gonzaga by 13 in the first half. It blitzed La Salle with a 17-3 start.

"We had energy from the get-go," Cotton said. "We wanted to come out and make a statement that we weren't going to bow down to nobody."

WSU weathered — or didn't need to weather — the Buckeyes' surge early in the second half. While the Shockers prepared for it, it never happened. They scored the first six points of the second half to build a 41-25 lead. Armstead's three made it 44-27 within inside 15 minutes remaining.

Ohio State made it push midway the half. Ross scored 10 of Ohio State's 12 points in a burst that got it within 56-43.

WSU's offense stalled and Early went to the locker room for X-rays after landing awkwardly on his left ankle. He returned minutes later, with WSU holding a 56-45 lead.

His return paid off quickly with his steal of pass by Ross. That led to a three-point play for VanVleet and a 60-45 lead with 7:03 remaining.

Ohio State responded with a 7-0 run that cut tiring WSU's lead to 60-52. It kept coming, getting within 62-57 before Tekele Cotton's three revived WSU momentarily.

Wichita State's offensive resurgence continued in the first half. The Shockers made 5 of 12 three-pointers and led 35-22 at halftime.

"Our first half was probably the worst I have seen us play in a very long time," Ohio State's Lenzelle Smith Jr. said. "They came out and fought from the jump ball."

Its defense maintained its season-long status. Ohio State, denied driving lanes and post shots, shot contested jumpers and missed. It finished the half 8 of 33 from the field and 2 of 10 from behind the arc. Thomas made 4 of 13 shots and missed all five of his threes.

BOX SCORE

Wichita State 70 • 30-8

##	Player	Total FG-FGA	3-Ptr FG-FGA	FT-FTA	Off	Def	Tot	PF	TP	A	TO	Blk	Stl	Min
11	Early, Cleanthony f	5-9	2-5	0-1	2	5	7	3	12	0	1	2	1	32
22	Hall, Carl f	3-8	0-0	2-2	2	2	4	3	8	0	1	6	1	27
02	Armstead, Malcolm g	6-21	2-6	0-0	1	6	7	4	14	3	3	0	3	37
31	Baker, Ron g	0-3	0-1	9-9	0	4	4	3	9	1	2	1	0	33
32	Cotton, Tekele g	2-6	2-3	4-8	3	2	5	4	10	1	2	0	1	30
00	Lufile, Chadrack	0-0	0-0	0-0	0	0	0	0	0	0	0	0	0	3
05	Williams, Demetric	1-1	1-1	0-0	0	1	1	1	3	2	0	0	0	7
21	Orukpe, Ehimen	1-2	0-0	0-0	2	0	2	2	2	0	1	0	0	5
23	VanVleet, Fred	4-8	1-3	3-3	0	3	3	3	12	2	1	0	2	24
50	White, Jake	0-1	0-1	0-0	0	1	1	0	0	0	1	0	0	2
	Team				3	3	6							
	Totals	22-59	8-20	18-23	13	27	40	23	70	9	12	9	8	200

FG % 1st Half: 11-31 35.5% 2nd half: 11-28 39.3% Game: 22-59 37.3%
3FG % 1st Half: 5-12 41.7% 2nd half: 3-8 37.5% Game: 8-20 40.0%
FT % 1st Half: 8-9 88.9% 2nd half: 10-14 71.4% Game: 18-23 78.3%

Deadball Rebounds 3,6

Ohio State 66 • 29-8

##	Player	Total FG-FGA	3-Ptr FG-FGA	FT-FTA	Off	Def	Tot	PF	TP	A	TO	Blk	Stl	Min
01	Thomas, Deshaun f	8-20	0-6	7-9	1	4	5	4	23	3	5	2	0	37
12	Thompson, Sam f	1-3	0-2	2-3	0	2	2	3	4	0	0	1	0	33
23	Williams, Amir c	0-0	0-0	0-0	0	3	3	1	0	0	0	4	0	17
04	Craft, Aaron g	2-12	2-7	3-5	0	7	7	4	9	2	2	0	2	38
32	Smith Jr., Lenzelle g	2-6	1-2	0-0	1	2	3	5	5	0	0	0	1	23
03	Scott, Shannon	2-7	0-1	2-2	5	2	7	2	6	2	0	0	0	25
10	Ross, LaQuinton	4-12	2-7	9-10	0	5	5	1	19	0	1	1	2	22
30	Ravenel, Evan	0-1	0-0	0-0	1	1	2	2	0	0	1	0	0	5
	Team				3	0	3							
	Totals	19-61	5-25	23-29	11	26	37	22	66	7	9	8	5	200

FG % 1st Half: 8-33 24.2% 2nd half: 11-28 39.3% Game: 19-61 31.1%
3FG % 1st Half: 2-10 20.0% 2nd half: 3-15 20.0% Game: 5-25 20.0%
FT % 1st Half: 4-7 57.1% 2nd half: 19-22 86.4% Game: 23-29 79.3%

Deadball Rebounds 4

Officials: Jamie Luckie, Patrick Adams, Raymond Natili
Technical fouls: Wichita State-None. Ohio State-None.
Attendance: 17998
2013 NCAA Men's DI Basketball West Regional Final

Score by periods	1st	2nd	Total
Wichita State	35	35	**70**
Ohio State	22	44	**66**

	Points	In Paint	Off T/O	2nd Chance	Fast Break	Bench
WSU		22	9	12	0	17
OSU		24	6	12	0	25

Last FG - WSU 2nd-01:00, OSU 2nd-00:08.
Largest lead - WSU by 20 2nd-12:39, OSU by 2 1st-14:07.

Score tied - 1 time.
Lead changed - 2 times.

Wichita State's Tekele Cotton is fouled while going up for a shot against Ohio State's Aaron Craft.
By Travis Heying, Wichita Eagle

LOUISVILLE 72
WICHITA STATE 68

JOURNEY'S END
LATE LOUISVILLE PRESSURE QUICKLY SHRINKS LEAD, HANDS WICHITA STATE SEMIFINAL LOSS

BY PAUL SUELLENTROP

ATLANTA -- The college basketball world kept waiting for the stage to get too big, for the scene to overwhelm Wichita State.

It never did, even as the lead slipped away in Saturday's NCAA national semifinal in the Georgia Dome. The ninth-seeded Shockers proved they belonged in the Final Four, which must make what happened more painful. The Shockers controlled most of the game and a spot in Monday's championship game awaited, a few minutes away.

"We felt like we had the game won," WSU guard Fred VanVleet said.

"When we were up 12, it felt really comfortable," teammate Ron Baker said.

So close to extending three weekends of superb basketball another two days, so close to playing for the school's first NCAA basketball title.

Louisville, however, ended that dream with a closing push that wore down the Shockers. The

Wichita State forward Carl Hall defends Louisville Cardinals forward Chane Behanan during the national semifinal game. *By Jaime Green, Wichita Eagle*

Wichita State's Ron Baker and Louisville's Luke Hancock tangle in the final seconds. A jump ball was called though Baker argued Hancock didn't have the ball. *By Jaime Green, Wichita Eagle*

Cardinals, down 12 in the second half, defeated WSU 72-68.

Louisville (34-5) plays in Monday's title game in search of the school's third NCAA title. WSU (30-9) must be satisfied - hard as it is to say - with a history-making run that came up a few turnovers and few minutes short of playing for No. 1.

"This one's especially hard because of the run we went on," WSU coach Gregg Marshall said. "This may be the most important game that I'll ever coach. It's probably the most important that Wichita State's ever played in."

The Shockers lived up to that for more than 30 minutes. For most of the game, Wichita State made Louisville's press look like little more than a nuisance. The Shockers calmly worked the ball up court, foiling the pressure with several ball-handlers, and took away Louisville's source of offense. The Shockers committed four turnovers in the game's first seven minutes. Then it didn't commit another one until seven minutes remained.

"Pressing teams have to stay in there," Louisville coach Rick Pitino said. "We started making some steals, picking up the heat."

Cleanthony Early led WSU with 24 points, making 8 of 14 shots. Carl Hall added 13. Malcolm Armstead, who averaged 15.5 points in four tournament games, scored two and missed 9 of 10 shots.

Russ Smith led Louisville with 21 points. Luke Hancock added 20, making 3 of 5 threes. He scored 14 points in the second half.

Left: Wichita State's Cleanthony Early goes to the basket in the second half against Louisville.
By Travis Heying, Wichita Eagle

Following Page: The Wichita State bench cheers after a Cleanthony Early three-pointer during the national semifinal game.
By Jaime Green, Wichita Eagle

WSU led by 12 points with 13:36 remaining and the Cardinals cut that lead in half in just over a minute. WSU pushed it back to eight points, briefly, and Louisville kept coming. It trailed 55-53 when three players engulfed Carl Hall and knocked the ball away, leading to a three-pointer by Luke Hancock for a 56-55 lead with 6:30 remaining.

The Cardinals forced seven turnovers in the final seven minutes and scored nine points off those turnovers.

"We made our run late," Louisville guard Peyton Siva said. "That's the trademark of our team."

The Cardinals turned it over to Hancock in the final minutes. His three-pointer gave them a 65-60 lead at the two-minute mark. His driving layup restored a five-point edge, 67-62.

He also made one of the game's biggest defensive plays by tying up Baker, after a missed free throw, with 6.3 seconds remaining. The possession arrow went Louisville's way, denying WSU the ball down three points.

Baker, who rebounded and then needed to dribble to gain his balance, thought he got rid of the ball to Armstead in time to avoid the jump ball. The referees disagreed and the Cardinals inbounded the ball to Smith, who made a free throw with 4.9 seconds to play for the final margin.

Early, a junior, came up big on the biggest stage. He grabbed 10 rebounds and scored 15 of his points in the second half. In the final minutes, he kept the Shockers close with his offensive rebounding.

His tip made it 67-64. Smith made a foul shot for a 68-64 lead with 45 seconds remaining. Early tipped in another miss to make it 68-66 with 31.6 seconds to play. Smith made two more free throws with 29.9 seconds to play for a four-point edge. Baker missed an off-balance three and Hall rebounded and scored to cut the margin to 70-68.

IT'S AN AGONIZING FINISH TO AN AMAZING STORY

BY BOB LUTZ

ATLANTA -- Maybe all Wichita State needed was one shot.

Maybe if that jump ball hadn't been called with six seconds remaining, the Shockers would have found a hero to make a three-pointer and send its national semifinal game against Louisville on Saturday into overtime.

"It would have been nice to have gotten a shot," WSU coach Gregg Marshall said.

Instead, the possession arrow went right through Wichita State's heart.

Louisville got the ball out of bounds, made a free-throw to get its lead to four, and beat a Wichita State team that gave its fans and its city a century's worth of memories in three weeks.

The jump ball call will be debated. It happened after Luke Hancock made the front end of a one-and-one for a three-point Louisville lead, then missed the second.

Left: Wichita State huddles together at the start of their national semifinal game against Louisville. *By Jaime Green, Wichita Eagle*

Above: Wichita State forward Carl Hall and Ron Baker wait for a rebound during a free throw in the final seconds of the national semifinal game. *By Jaime Green, Wichita Eagle*

The ball bounced hard off the rim and WSU's Ron Baker made the grab. But he was off balance, so he had to dribble so as not to travel. With the ball at Baker's waist level, Hancock reached in and, the officials ruled, had the tie up long enough.

Every eye in the massive Georgia Dome shot toward the possession arrow. Louisville exhaled when it saw where it was pointed; Wichita State cringed.

The Shockers played the first 27 minutes like a national champion. Cleanthony Early's three-pointer with 13:41 to play put them up by 12. By 12, mind you, over the tournament's top seed,

a Cardinals team that had won 14 straight and toyed with some of the most dangerous teams in college basketball.

Where did it go wrong for the Shockers?

It started when they allowed Louisville junior Tim Henderson, whose parents probably passed out when he went into the game because of how little he's played this season, made back-to-back three-pointers to cut that 12-point lead in half.

It was a shock to WSU's system to see Henderson, who played a season-high 10 minutes, act as Louisville's defibrillator.

From that point, there was no more running and hiding from the Cardinals. The soft butter

pressure defense the Cardinals had been employing became a brick wall. During a seven-possession stretch, Wichita State committed five turnovers, nearly half of what the Shockers had in the game.

WSU's lead continued to melt. Louisville, as most expected, won 72-68.

And the Shockers lost the kind of game that will cause Marshall, his assistants and the team's players many sleepless nights.

They'll pick this one apart, looking for reasons, searching for a turning point.

"This may be the most important basketball game that I'll ever coach," Marshall said.

As his players tried to answer questions on the podium after the game, Marshall stared straight ahead. It was a stark contrast to the post-game interview session after the Shockers knocked off Ohio State last Saturday to reach their first Final Four in 48 years.

As players talked then, Marshall was checking his phone for the 500 or so congratulatory text messages he was getting, one after another.

Saturday, though, he looked ashen. The suddenness of the craziest and best ride in the history of Shocker basketball being over was jolting, almost unbearable. Even against Louisville, the team most are picking to win the national championship.

It's nice that legendary Cardinals coach Rick Pitino has been leading the cheers for Shocker basketball all week. He continued after Saturday's game.

"Last year we played the No. 1 RPI schedule in the nation and this year we played a top-five schedule," Pitino said. "I don't think we could face a basketball team any better than Wichita State. They are great."

Pitino isn't trying to win friends when he says things like that.

The Shockers can be great. At times Saturday they were great. But they weren't great in the final 13 minutes, when they most needed to be.

WSU outscored Louisville 17-7 to start the second half. When they were up 12, it was difficult to imagine a scenario in which the Cardinals could come back.

And then Henderson, a junior who had played a grand total of 208 minutes in his Louisville career, made two huge shots from the corner. The same Henderson who made a mop-up three-pointer to close out an 85-63 Elite Eight win over Duke last week.

That would have been a good enough story to tell his grandchildren someday. But he topped it big-time against Wichita State.

Henderson's pair of treys served as a wake-up call for the Cardinals and put doubt in the minds of the Shockers. Things had been going so swimmingly, and then a kid whose father is a former Louisville swimmer makes the 10th and 11th three-pointers of his career.

Henderson's shot were the beginning of a 37-21 Louisville barrage in the final 13 minutes. The Cardinals had scored 35 in the first 27.

So, yes, getting the ball for one final shot would have been nice. And the Shockers might have done something historic with that possession. We'll never know.

What we do know is that Wichita State could have gone farther in this tournament. They could have been playing for a championship Monday night, with apologies to no one.

What an incredible season. It ended in a difficult way, but the Shockers will pick up these pieces. Marshall, so deflated by the loss, also talked about how excited he is about the future.

There are no guarantees WSU will be on this stage again. It's such a hard feat to accomplish. But the Shockers are in position to be good year after year.

Cleanthony Early, who looked like a future NBA player with his 24 points and 10 rebounds against Louisville, will be back next season. So will Ron Baker, Tekele Cotton, Fred VanVleet and others.

"This is just a beginning," Marshall said.

But the end still hurts.

Shocker senior Carl Hall shoots over Louisville center Gorgui Dieng in the national semifinal.
By Jaime Green, Wichita Eagle

Above: Louisville's Luke Hancock reaches above WSU's Ron Baker for a rebound in the first half.
By Travis Heying, Wichita Eagle

Facing Page: Wichita State's Cleanthony Early celebrates after getting fouled in the second half against Louisville.
By Travis Heying, Wichita Eagle

M MICHIGAN

NCAA.com

CELEBRATING 75 YEARS

Previous Page: More than 75,000 fans watched Wichita State face Louisville in the national semifinal in the Georgia Dome.
By Jaime Green, Wichita Eagle

Right: WuShock and the rest of the Wichita State party traveled to five games over 16 days in three time zones.
By Jaime Green, Wichita Eagle

BOX SCORE

WICHITA STATE 68 • 30-9

##	Player		Total FG-FGA	3-Ptr FG-FGA	FT-FTA	Off	Def	Tot	PF	TP	A	TO	Blk	Stl	Min
11	Early, Cleanthony	f	8-14	2-4	6-7	4	6	10	3	24	0	0	1	0	37
22	Hall, Carl	f	4-5	0-0	5-7	3	2	5	2	13	0	2	0	2	30
02	Armstead, Malcolm	g	1-10	0-5	0-0	1	3	4	4	2	7	3	0	2	29
31	Baker, Ron	g	3-9	3-6	2-2	2	6	8	4	11	0	1	0	0	33
32	Cotton, Tekele	g	4-9	1-2	0-0	3	1	4	3	9	2	1	0	1	27
00	Lufile, Chadrack		1-1	0-0	0-0	0	1	1	0	2	0	0	0	0	3
05	Williams, Demetric		0-0	0-0	0-0	0	0	0	0	0	1	0	0	0	7
15	Wiggins, Nick		1-2	0-1	0-0	0	0	0	0	2	0	0	0	0	1
21	Orukpe, Ehimen		0-0	0-0	0-2	0	2	2	2	0	0	0	0	0	7
23	VanVleet, Fred		0-4	0-2	3-4	0	1	1	1	3	3	3	0	0	23
50	White, Jake		0-0	0-0	2-2	0	0	0	1	2	0	0	0	0	3
	Team					1	0	1				1			
	Totals		22-54	6-20	18-24	14	22	36	20	68	13	11	1	5	200

FG % 1st Half: 9-28 32.1% 2nd half: 13-26 50.0% Game: 22-54 40.7%
3FG % 1st Half: 3-10 30.0% 2nd half: 3-10 30.0% Game: 6-20 30.0%
FT % 1st Half: 5-6 83.3% 2nd half: 13-18 72.2% Game: 18-24 75.0%
Deadball Rebounds 1

LOUISVILLE 72 • 34-5

##	Player		Total FG-FGA	3-Ptr FG-FGA	FT-FTA	Off	Def	Tot	PF	TP	A	TO	Blk	Stl	Min
20	BLACKSHEAR, Wayne	f	0-1	0-1	0-0	0	1	1	3	0	0	0	0	0	9
21	BEHANAN, Chane	f	3-5	0-0	4-4	5	4	9	3	10	1	0	0	1	29
10	DIENG, Gorgui	c	0-1	0-0	0-0	0	6	6	4	0	0	1	2	0	30
02	SMITH, Russ	g	6-17	4-11	5-12	1	1	2	3	21	3	5	0	2	36
03	SIVA, Peyton	g	1-9	0-5	5-6	0	1	1	1	7	3	2	0	2	34
11	HANCOCK, Luke		6-9	3-5	5-7	1	3	4	2	20	2	0	0	2	31
15	HENDERSON, Tim		2-3	2-3	0-0	0	2	2	2	6	0	0	0	0	10
24	HARRELL, Montrezl		4-4	0-0	0-0	3	1	4	2	8	1	0	0	1	11
44	VAN TREESE, Stephan		0-0	0-0	0-0	1	2	3	3	0	0	0	1	1	10
	Team					0	1	1							
	Totals		22-49	9-25	19-29	11	22	33	23	72	10	9	3	8	200

FG % 1st Half: 8-20 40.0% 2nd half: 14-29 48.3% Game: 22-49 44.9%
3FG % 1st Half: 4-13 30.8% 2nd half: 5-12 41.7% Game: 9-25 36.0%
FT % 1st Half: 5-9 55.6% 2nd half: 14-20 70.0% Game: 19-29 65.5%
Deadball Rebounds 4,1

Officials: Les Jones, Karl Hess, Terry Wymer
Technical fouls: WICHITA STATE-None. LOUISVILLE-None.
Attendance:
2013 NCAA National Semifinal

Score by periods	1st	2nd	Total
WICHITA STATE	26	42	**68**
LOUISVILLE	25	47	**72**

WICHITA STATE SEASON STATS

Wichita State Basketball
Wichita State Season Box Score (as of Apr 06, 2013)
All games

RECORD:

	OVERALL	HOME	AWAY	NEUTRAL
ALL GAMES.........	(30-9)	(15-2)	(7-5)	(8-2)
CONFERENCE........	(12-6)	(7-2)	(5-4)	(0-0)
NON-CONFERENCE......	(18-3)	(8-0)	(2-1)	(8-2)

## Player	GP-GS	Min	Avg	FG-FGA	Pct	3FG-FGA	Pct	FT-FTA	Pct	Off	Def	Tot	Avg	PF	FO	A	TO	Blk	Stl	Pts	Avg
11 Cleanthony Early..	39-22	979	25.1	184-404	.455	47-148	.318	129-163	.791	89	123	212	5.4	100	3	23	61	35	29	544	13.9
22 Hall, Carl.......	32-26	916	28.6	145-267	.543	0-2	.000	111-165	.673	101	117	218	6.8	75	0	22	43	55	16	401	12.5
02 Armstead, Malcolm..	39-39	1114	28.6	147-373	.394	61-177	.345	61-76	.803	29	121	150	3.8	90	0	157	89	2	76	416	10.7
31 Baker, Ron......	18-15	469	26.1	45-113	.398	30-84	.357	37-45	.822	22	36	58	2.5	39	0	32	23	5	14	157	8.7
05 Williams, Demetric.	39-26	973	24.9	97-252	.385	32-114	.281	62-81	.765	16	82	98	2.5	84	2	87	63	1	44	288	7.4
32 Cotton, Tekele..	39-28	923	23.7	92-209	.440	24-66	.364	44-82	.537	57	96	153	3.9	81	1	67	44	6	40	252	6.5
03 Wessel, Evan......	8-8	152	19.0	16-33	.485	11-24	.458	1-1	1.000	4	10	14	1.8	15	0	15	5	1	2	44	5.5
15 Wiggins, Nick....	36-1	461	12.8	59-135	.437	31-74	.419	27-37	.730	12	51	63	1.8	29	0	11	21	6	10	176	4.9
23 VanVleet, Fred..	39-0	630	16.2	59-153	.386	20-49	.408	29-40	.725	13	59	72	1.8	43	1	89	46	2	35	167	4.3
50 White, Jake.....	37-0	402	10.9	51-109	.468	3-27	.111	17-37	.730	33	74	107	2.9	49	0	10	28	0	7	132	3.6
21 Orukpe, Ehimen..	36-30	545	15.1	39-83	.470	0-0	.000	17-44	.386	57	100	157	4.4	73	0	8	46	56	11	95	2.6
00 Lufile, Chadrack...	30-0	236	7.9	20-35	.571	0-0	.000	8-20	.400	16	37	53	1.8	22	0	9	12	8	5	48	1.6
TEAM........										63	79	142	3.6	0			11				
Total.........	39	7800		954-2166	.440	259-765	.339	553-791	.699	512	985	1497	38.4	700	7	530	492	177	289	2720	69.7
Opponents......	39	7799		797-2020	.395	238-739	.322	553-774	.714	355	835	1190	30.5	703	-	410	505	116	220	2385	61.2

SCORE BY PERIODS:

	1st	2nd	Total
Wichita State..............	1228	1492	2720
Opponents.................	1060	1325	2385

DEADBALL REBOUNDS:

	OFF	DEF	TOTAL
Wichita State..............	97	11	108
Opponents.................	93	7	100

WICHITA STATE SEASON RESULTS

Date	Opponent	Result	Leading scorer
Nov. 10	N.C.-Central	W,71-57	Ron Baker (18)
Nov. 13	at VCU	W,53-51	Cleanthony Early (13)
Nov. 15	Western Carolina	W,79-63	Cleanthony Early (21)
Nov. 17	Howard	W,69-50	Demetric Williams (11) Carl Hall (11)
Nov. 20	x-DePaul	W,75-62	Demetric Williams (18)
Nov. 21	x-Iowa	W,75-63	Cleanthony Early (25)
Nov. 28	Tulsa	W,86-60	Carl Hall (16)
Dec. 2	at Air Force	W,72-69	Carl Hall (21)
Dec. 8	Northern Colorado	W,80-54	Cleanthony Early (16)
Dec. 13	at Tennessee	L,69-60	Carl Hall (21)
Dec. 20	Charleston Southern	W,65-53	Cleanthony Early (20)
Dec. 22	y-Southern Miss	W,59-51	Demetric Williams (17)
Dec. 30	Northern Iowa	W,66-41	Cleanthony Early (16)
Jan. 2	at Drake	W,75-63	Nick Wiggins (18)
Jan. 6	at Bradley	W,69-63	Cleanthony Early (16)
Jan. 9	Southern Illinois	W,82-76	Cleanthony Early (39)
Jan. 13	at Evansville	L,71-67	Malcolm Armstead (21)
Jan. 16	Illinois St.	W,74-62	Cleanthony Early (16)
Jan. 19	Creighton	W,67-64	Carl Hall (17)
Jan. 23	at Missouri St.	W,62-52	Cleanthony Early (17)
Jan. 26	Bradley	W,73-39	Nick Wiggins (12)
Jan. 29	Indiana St.	L,68-55	Cleanthony Early (15)
Feb. 2	at Northern Iowa	L,57-52	Carl Hall (20)
Feb. 5	at Southern Illinois	L,64-62	Demetric Williams (15)
Feb. 9	Missouri St.	W,79-50	Cleanthony Early (16)
Feb. 13	Drake	W,71-56	Fred VanVleet (17)
Feb. 17	at Illinois St.	W,68-67	Malcolm Armstead (18)
Feb. 19	at Indiana St.	W,66-62	Cleanthony Early (19)
Feb. 23	Detroit	W,94-79	Malcolm Armstead (20)
Feb. 27	Evansville	L,59-56	Tekele Cotton (12)
March 2	at Creighton	L,91-79	Demetric Williams (18)
March 8	z-Missouri St.	W,69-59	Carl Hall (18)
March 9	z-Illinois St.	W,66-51	Carl Hall (16)
March 10	z-Creighton	L68-65	Malcolm Armstead (28)
March 21	a-Pittsburgh	W,73-55	Malcolm Armstead (22)
March 23	a-Gonzaga	W,76-70	Ron Baker (16) Cleanthony Early (16)
March 28	b-La Salle	W,72-56	Malcolm Armstead (18)
March 30	b-Ohio St.	W,70-66	Malcolm Armstead (14)
April 6	c-Louisville	L,72-68	Cleanthony Early (24)

x-at Cancun, Mexico
y-at Intrust Bank Arena
z-MVC tournament at St. Louis
a-NCAA Tournament at Salt Lake City
b-NCAA Tournament at Los Angeles
c-NCAA national semifinal at Atlanta

CONGRATULATIONS SHOCKERS

we're proud of you!

FOOD STORES®